Learning Karaf Cellar

Build and implement a complete clustering solution
for the Apache Karaf OSGi container

Jean-Baptiste Onofré

PUBLISHING

BIRMINGHAM - MUMBAI

Learning Karaf Cellar

Copyright © 2014 Packt Publishing

First published: July 2014

Production reference: 1150714

Published by Packt Publishing Ltd.
Livery Place
35 Livery Street
Birmingham B3 2PB, UK.

ISBN 978-1-78398-460-2

www.packtpub.com

Cover image by Abhinav Pandey (abhinavphotography30@gmail.com)

Credits

Author
Jean-Baptiste Onofré

Reviewers
Ladislav Gažo
Sachin Handiekar
Achim Nierbeck

Commissioning Editor
Usha Iyer

Acquisition Editor
Meeta Rajani

Content Development Editor
Susmita Panda Sabat

Technical Editors
Mrunal Chavan
Ankita Jha
Pankaj Kadam

Copy Editors
Alisha Aranha
Roshni Banerjee
Dipti Kapadia
Aditya Nair
Karuna Narayanan

Project Coordinator
Neha Thakur

Proofreaders
Simran Bhogal
Ameesha Green
Paul Hindle

Indexers
Hemangini Bari
Tejal Soni

Graphics
Ronak Dhruv
Valentina D'silva

Production Coordinator
Nilesh R. Mohite

Cover Work
Nilesh R. Mohite

About the Author

Jean-Baptiste Onofré is a member of the Apache Software Foundation, and he has been involved in Apache projects for the past 10 years. He is the PMC chair of Apache Karaf and its subprojects, including Cellar, Cave, and EIK.

He is also a PMC member of Apache ACE, Apache ServiceMix, and Apache Syncope, and he is a committer for Apache ActiveMQ, Apache Archiva, Apache Aries, Apache Camel, and Apache jClouds.

He is currently working for Talend (http://www.talend.com) as a software architect and is a member of the Talend Apache team.

He writes articles on Java technologies for *Linux Magazine France* and has worked as a reviewer for *Apache ServiceMix How-To, Henryk Konsek*, and *Learning Apache Karaf, Johan Edstrom, Jamie Goodyear, and Heath Kesler*. Both of these books are published by Packt Publishing. He is currently reviewing *Apache Karaf Cookbook, Johan Edstrom, Jamie Goodyear, Heath Kesler, and Achim Nierbeck, Packt Publishing*.

He has also given speeches about Apache projects (Karaf, Camel, and so on) at different conferences, especially at ApacheCon NA, ApacheCon Europe, and CamelOne.

I would like to thank the whole Karaf team, especially Guillaume Nodet, Achim Nierbeck, Jamie Goodyear, Ioannis Canellos, and all others. We are a great team, and you all do a great job.

I would also like to thank my wife, Lucile, who accepted that I spent some nights on this book.

About the Reviewers

Ladislav Gažo is a computer enthusiast who has been digging into the software world for a long time. He has professional experience of more than 12 years in development and software engineering. While starting experiments with computer graphics and network administration, he realized that the true path is towards the combination of software engineering and business. He has been developing, analyzing, and architecting Java-based, desktop-based, and finally modern web-based solutions for several years. The application of the Agile approach and advanced technology is both a hobby and a day-to-day job.

Rich experience with various technologies led him to co-found the company Seges Ltd., which is a software development company in Slovakia. He actively participates in start-up events and helps to build development communities such as Google Developer Group and Java User Group in Slovakia. With his colleagues, he has designed and released an interactive content management solution called Synapso, which utilizes contemporary technologies with user experience in mind.

> I would not be able to materialize my knowledge as part of the review process of this book without the support of all my colleagues, friends, and family. Creating a good long-term environment helped me to gain the experience that I can pass on further.

Sachin Handiekar is a Senior Software Developer with over five years of experience in Java EE development. He is a graduate in Computer Science from the University of Greenwich, London, and he currently works for a global consulting company that develops enterprise applications using various open source technologies such as Apache Camel, ServiceMix, ActiveMQ, and ZooKeeper.

He has a lot of interest in open source projects and has contributed code to Apache Camel as well as developed plugins for Spring Social, which can be found on GitHub at `https://github.com/sachin-handiekar`.

He also actively writes about enterprise application development on his blog (`http://sachinhandiekar.com`).

Achim Nierbeck has more than 14 years of experience in designing and implementing Java enterprise applications. He is a committer and PMC at Apache Karaf and is the project lead of the OPS4J Pax Web projects. Since 2010, he has enjoyed working on OSGi enterprise applications. He is one of the authors of *Apache Karaf Cookbook* by Packt Publishing (yet to be published).

While not working on projects or open source development, he enjoys spending time with his family and friends. He can be reached at `notizblog.nierbeck.de`.

www.PacktPub.com

Support files, eBooks, discount offers, and more

You might want to visit www.PacktPub.com for support files and downloads related to your book.

Did you know that Packt offers eBook versions of every book published, with PDF and ePub files available? You can upgrade to the eBook version at www.PacktPub.com and as a print book customer, you are entitled to a discount on the eBook copy. Get in touch with us at service@packtpub.com for more details.

At www.PacktPub.com, you can also read a collection of free technical articles, sign up for a range of free newsletters and receive exclusive discounts and offers on Packt books and eBooks.

http://PacktLib.PacktPub.com

Do you need instant solutions to your IT questions? PacktLib is Packt's online digital book library. Here, you can access, read and search across Packt's entire library of books.

Why subscribe?

- Fully searchable across every book published by Packt
- Copy and paste, print and bookmark content
- On demand and accessible via web browser

Free access for Packt account holders

If you have an account with Packt at www.PacktPub.com, you can use this to access PacktLib today and view nine entirely free books. Simply use your login credentials for immediate access.

Table of Contents

Preface	**1**
Chapter 1: Apache Karaf – Provisioning and Clusters	**7**
What is OSGi?	**8**
The OSGi framework	8
The OSGi bundle	9
Dependency between bundles	9
The OSGi container	**11**
Provisioning in Apache Karaf	13
OBR	15
Apache Karaf Features	15
Multiple Apache Karaf containers	**17**
Provisioning clusters	19
Summary	**20**
Chapter 2: Apache Karaf Cellar	**21**
Cluster topologies	**21**
Apache Karaf Cellar architecture	**24**
Apache Karaf Cellar installation and first commands	**26**
Cluster resources	**27**
Bundles	27
Karaf features	30
Configuration	33
Optional resources	36
The Karaf WebConsole plugin	37
Summary	**38**
Chapter 3: Hazelcast	**39**
What is Hazelcast?	**39**
Distributed cluster resource states	**40**
Distributed queues and topics	41

The Cellar distributed map   42
Replicas/Backup   **42**
Persistence   43
Networks   **44**
Multiple clusters   44
TCP/IP   45
Interfaces   45
SSL   46
Encryption   47
IPv6 support   48
Restricting outbound ports   49
Summary   **50**

Chapter 4: Cluster Groups   **51**
Managing cluster groups   **51**
Targeting provisioning   **53**
Features   54
Bundles   55
Configurations   57
Optional resources   57
Overlapping   58
The summary of commands   59
Summary   **60**

Chapter 5: Producers, Consumers, Handlers, Listeners, and Synchronizers   **61**
The event producer   **62**
The event consumer   **63**
Event handlers   **64**
Listeners and synchronizers   **67**
Summary   **68**

Chapter 6: The Filtering of Cluster Events   **69**
The configuration of the filters   **69**
Resources   **70**
Blacklist and whitelist   **71**
Inbound and outbound   **71**
Regex and event identification   **71**
Bundle   72
Configuration   73
Features   74
The default filter configuration   **75**
Summary   **76**

Chapter 7: DOSGi   77

  What is Cellar DOSGi?   77
  The API bundle   79
  The service bundle   81
  The client bundle   84
  Summary   86

Chapter 8: Cellar and Camel   87

  The communication between remote routes   87
  Caching with a distributed map   91
  Summary   93

Chapter 9: Roadmap   95

  HTTP load balancing and session clustering   95
    Load balancing   96
    Session clustering   99
  Clustering a log service   100
  Summary   101

Index   103

Preface

Apache Karaf has been emerging as the main container for the Open Software Gateway initiative (OSGi) applications. This is mainly because more and more people can see the benefits of OSGi in terms of the reuse of components, versioning, and reduced complexity with real modular applications.

People are also looking for a ready-to-use container that provides all the features expected in a mission-critical and enterprise-ready environment: management, monitoring, and provisioning. It's what Karaf provides, simplifying the development, execution, and production of OSGi applications. However, Karaf is more than a container focused on OSGi; even though it's powered by OSGi, it also supports non-OSGi applications such as Spring or web applications.

In modern architecture, most of the time, we don't have a single instance of the container to be running. In order to provide scalability and high availability, a classic architecture contains multiple container instances that form a farm or cluster of Karaf containers. This architecture brings up new questions: how do you deploy your application components on different instances? How can you target this deployment only on a subset of nodes for staging purposes, for instance? How can you deal with the configuration on different nodes?

Apache Karaf Cellar has been created to address these questions and many more questions.

This book will begin by giving you the means to understand OSGi and Apache Karaf as well as the concepts of a provisioning cluster. By doing so, it will provide the baseline needed before you shift to the advanced usage of Cellar, such as cluster groups or the filtering of cluster events.

This book details the Cellar architecture and the different commands provided by Cellar, from the installation up to the management of clusters.

More than a simple provisioning or synchronization cluster, this book will show you the Cellar runtime features such as Distributed OSGi (DOSGi) and interaction with Apache Camel to create a multinode integration platform.

Using this book, readers will get a detailed understanding, through how-to steps, to set up a cluster of Karaf nodes.

What this book covers

Chapter 1, Apache Karaf – Provisioning and Clusters, reviews what an OSGi is, the purposes, architectures, and components. We will introduce details about the Apache Karaf container, its architecture, and features. We will also introduce the question of how to manage multiple Apache Karaf instances.

Chapter 2, Apache Karaf Cellar, introduces Apache Karaf Cellar and the different cluster topologies that it can address. After the presentation of the Cellar architecture, we will perform our first cluster installation and manage different resources on the cluster using different techniques to monitor the current cluster state.

Chapter 3, Hazelcast, digs into the Cellar engine. After the introduction of Hazelcast, we will see different configurations that are useful for Cellar, especially around the network setup.

Chapter 4, Cluster Groups, shows you how to set up cluster groups in Cellar, allowing you to create a subset of nodes and target provisioning.

Chapter 5, Producers, Consumers, Handlers, Listeners, and Synchronizers, introduces you to the Cellar components used for the production, consumption, and transportation of cluster events between different nodes in a cluster.

Chapter 6, The Filtering of Cluster Events, shows you how to filter cluster events, allowing a fine-grained configuration of the resource synchronization in a cluster.

Chapter 7, DOSGi, shows that Cellar is not just a provisioning and synchronization clustering solution by introducing the first runtime clustering feature provided by Cellar: DOSGi. We will see how to use Cellar to implement remote communication between bundles located on different nodes using an example.

Chapter 8, Cellar and Camel, shows the second runtime clustering feature provided by Cellar by leveraging the camel-hazelcast component. Thanks to Cellar and Hazelcast, we will see how to implement remote communication between the Camel routes located on different nodes through an example.

Chapter 9, Roadmap, presents the new ideas and features that will come in the future versions of Cellar. This chapter gives an overview of the Cellar roadmap.

What you need for this book

In this book, the software required is as follows:

- Operating systems: Any system that supports Java:
  - ○ Windows XP or superior
  - ○ Unix (Linux, AIX, Solaris, and so on)
- Java JDK 1.7
- Apache Karaf Cellar 2.3.4

Who this book is for

This book is for developers and system administrators who want to implement a clustering solution for Apache Karaf. They will master and dominate Cellar from installation to advanced usage. Thanks to the first chapter, even if you are not familiar with Karaf, you will receive a comprehensive look at Apache Karaf before you jump into the details of clustering.

Conventions

In this book, you will find a number of styles of text that distinguish between different kinds of information. Here are some examples of these styles and an explanation of their meaning.

Code words in text, database table names, folder names, filenames, file extensions, pathnames, dummy URLs, user input, and Twitter handles are shown as follows: "You have to copy the JDBC driver JAR file into the lib/ext folder."

A block of code is set as follows:

```
karaf.lock=true
karaf.lock.class=org.apache.karaf.main.SimpleFileLock
karaf.lock.dir=/path/to/lockfile
karaf.lock.delay=10
```

Any command-line input or output is written as follows:

```
karaf@node1> config:edit my
karaf@node1> config:propset key other
karaf@node1> config:update
```

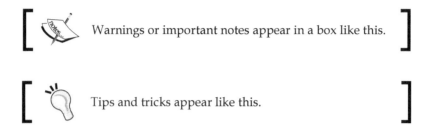

[Warnings or important notes appear in a box like this.]

[Tips and tricks appear like this.]

Reader feedback

Feedback from our readers is always welcome. Let us know what you think about this book—what you liked or may have disliked. Reader feedback is important for us to develop titles that you really get the most out of.

To send us general feedback, simply send an e-mail to feedback@packtpub.com, and mention the book title through the subject of your message.

If there is a topic that you have expertise in and you are interested in either writing or contributing to a book, see our author guide on www.packtpub.com/authors.

Customer support

Now that you are the proud owner of a Packt book, we have a number of things to help you to get the most from your purchase.

Downloading the example code

You can download the example code files for all Packt books you have purchased from your account at http://www.packtpub.com. If you purchased this book elsewhere, you can visit http://www.packtpub.com/support and register to have the files e-mailed directly to you.

Errata

Although we have taken every care to ensure the accuracy of our content, mistakes do happen. If you find a mistake in one of our books — maybe a mistake in the text or the code — we would be grateful if you would report this to us. By doing so, you can save other readers from frustration and help us improve subsequent versions of this book. If you find any errata, please report them by visiting http://www.packtpub.com/support, selecting your book, clicking on the **errata submission form** link, and entering the details of your errata. Once your errata are verified, your submission will be accepted and the errata will be uploaded to our website, or added to any list of existing errata, under the Errata section of that title.

Piracy

Piracy of copyright material on the Internet is an ongoing problem across all media. At Packt, we take the protection of our copyright and licenses very seriously. If you come across any illegal copies of our works, in any form, on the Internet, please provide us with the location address or website name immediately so that we can pursue a remedy.

Please contact us at copyright@packtpub.com with a link to the suspected pirated material.

We appreciate your help in protecting our authors, and our ability to bring you valuable content.

Questions

You can contact us at questions@packtpub.com if you are having a problem with any aspect of the book, and we will do our best to address it.

1
Apache Karaf – Provisioning and Clusters

Open Software Gateway initiative (OSGi) has been "hidden" for a long time and reserved to middleware such as IDE or application servers. However, OSGi can be applied in a lot of different contexts and applications. An OSGi application needs an environment to run. Apache Karaf is a lightweight, powerful, and enterprise-ready OSGi container where you can deploy your applications. On a production system, especially a mission-critical platform, it makes sense to be able to manage a set of Apache Karaf containers and to spread the deployment (or provisioning) of applications to these different instances.

In this chapter, we will cover the following topics:

- What is OSGi and what are its key features?
- The role of the OSGi framework
- The OSGi base artifact — the OSGi bundle and the concept of dependencies between bundles
- The Apache Karaf OSGi container and the provisioning of applications in the container
- How to manage the provisioning on multiple Karaf instances?

What is OSGi?

Developers are always looking for very dynamic, flexible, and agile software components. The purposes to do so are as follows:

- **Reuse**: This feature states that instead of duplicating the code, a component should be shared by other components, and multiple versions of the same component should be able to cohabit.

- **Visibility**: This feature specifies that a component should not use the implementation from another component directly. The implementation should be hidden, and the client module should use the interface provided by another component.

- **Agility**: This feature specifies that the deployment of a new version of a component should not require you to restart the platform. Moreover, a configuration change should not require a restart. For instance, it's not acceptable to restart a production platform just to change a log level. A *minor* change such as a log level should be dynamic, and the platform should be agile enough to reload the components that should be reloaded.

- **Discovery**: This feature states that a component should be able to discover other components. It's a kind of Plug and Play system: as soon as a component needs another component, it just looks for it and uses it.

OSGi has been created to address the preceding points.

The core concept is to force developers to use a very modular architecture in order to reduce complexity. As this paradigm is applicable for most modern systems, OSGi is now used for small embedded devices as well as for very large systems.

Different applications and systems use OSGi, for example, desktop applications, application servers, frameworks, embedded devices, and so on.

The OSGi framework

OSGi is designed to run in Java. In order to provide these features and deploy OSGi applications, a core layer has to be deployed in the **Java Virtual Machine (JVM)**: the OSGi framework.

This framework manages the life cycle and the relationship between the different OSGi components and artifacts.

The OSGi bundle

In OSGi, the components are packaged as OSGi bundles. An OSGi bundle is a simple Java **JAR (Java ARchive)** file that contains additional metadata used by the OSGi framework. These metadata are stored in the manifest file of the JAR file.

The following is the metadata:

```
Manifest-Version: 1.0
Bundle-ManifestVersion: 2
Bundle-Version: 2.1.6
Bundle-Name: My Logger
Bundle-SymbolicName: my_logger
Export-Package: org.my.osgi.logger;version=2.1
Import-Package: org.apache.log4j;version="[1.2,2)"
Private-Package: org.my.osgi.logger.internal
```

We can see that OSGi is very descriptive and verbose. We explicitly describe all the OSGi metadata (headers), including the package that we export or import with a specified version or version range.

As the OSGi headers are defined in the META-INF/MANIFEST file contained in the JAR file, it means that an OSGi bundle is a regular JAR file that you can use outside of OSGi.

The life cycle layer of the OSGi framework is an API to install, start, stop, update, and uninstall OSGi bundles.

Dependency between bundles

An OSGi bundle can use other bundles from the OSGi framework in two ways.

The first way is *static* code sharing. When we say that this bundle exports packages, it means a bundle can expose some code for other bundles. On the other hand, when we say that this bundle imports packages, it means a bundle can use code from other bundles.

For instance, we have the bundle A (packaged as the bundleA.jar file) with the following META-INF/MANIFEST file:

```
Manifest-Version: 1.0
Bundle-ManifestVersion: 2
Bundle-Version: 1.0.0
Bundle-Name: Bundle A
Bundle-SymbolicName: bundle_a
Export-Package: com.bundle.a;version=1.0
```

We can see that the bundle A exposes (exports) the `com.bundle.a` package with Version 1.0. On the other hand, we have the bundle B (packaged as the `bundleB.jar` file) with the following `META-INF/MANIIFEST` file:

```
Manifest-Version: 1.0
Bundle-ManifestVersion: 2
Bundle-Version: 2.0.0
Bundle-Name: Bundle B
Bundle-SymbolicName: bundle_b
Import-Package: com.bundle.a;version="[1.0,2)"
```

We can see that the bundle B imports (so, it will use) the `com.bundle.a` package in any version between 1.0 and 2 (excluded). So, this means that the OSGi framework will wire the bundles, as the bundle A provides the package used by the bundle B (so, the constraint is resolved).

This mechanism is similar to regular Java applications, but instead of embedding the required JAR files in your application, you can just declare the expected code. The OSGi framework is responsible for the link between the different bundles; it's done by the modules layer of the OSGi framework. This approach is interesting when you want to use code which is not natively designed for OSGi. It's a step forward for the reuse of components. However, it provides a limited answer to the purposes seen earlier in the chapter, especially visibility and discovery.

The second way in which an OSGi bundle can use other bundles from the OSGi framework is more interesting. It uses **Service-Oriented Architecture (SOA)** for low-level components. Here, more than exposing the code, an OSGi bundle exposes a OSGi service. On the other hand, another bundle can use an OSGi service. The services layer of the OSGi framework provides a service registry and all the plumbing mechanisms to wire the services.

The OSGi services provide a very dynamic system, offering a Publish-Find-Bind model for the bundles.

Downloading the example code

You can download the example code files for all Packt books you have purchased from your account at http://www.packtpub.com. If you purchased this book elsewhere, you can visit http://www.packtpub.com/support and register to have the files e-mailed directly to you.

The OSGi container

The OSGi container provides a set of additional features on top of the OSGi framework, as shown in the following diagram:

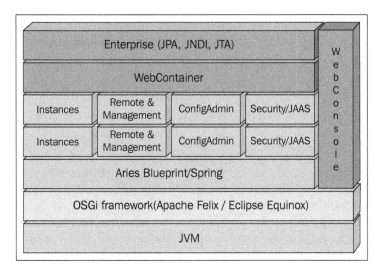

Apache Karaf provides the following features:

- It provides the abstraction of the OSGi framework. If you write an OSGi application, you have to package your application tightly coupled with the OSGi framework (such as the Apache Felix framework or Eclipse Equinox). Most of the time, you have to prepare the scripts, configuration files, and so on in order to provide a complete, ready-to-use application. Apache Karaf allows you to focus only on your application. Karaf, by default, provides the packaging (including scripts and so on), and it also abstracts the OSGi framework. Thanks to Karaf, it's very easy to switch from Apache Felix (the default framework in Karaf) to Eclipse Equinox.

- Provides support for the OSGi Blueprint and Spring frameworks. Apache Karaf allows you to directly use Blueprint or Spring as the dependency framework in your bundles. In the new version of Karaf (starting from Karaf 3.0.1), it also supports new dependency frameworks (such as DS, CDI, and so on).

- Apache Karaf provides a complete, Unix-like shell console where you have a lot of commands available to manage and monitor your running container. This shell console works on any system supporting Java and provides a complete Unix-like environment, including completion, contextual help, key bindings, and more. You can access the shell console using SSH. Apache Karaf also provides a complete management layer (using JMX) that is remotely accessible, which means you can perform the same actions as you do using the shell commands with several MBeans.

- In addition to the default root Apache Karaf container, for convenience, Apache Karaf allows you to manage multiple container instances. Apache Karaf provides dedicated commands and MBeans to create the instances, control the instances, and so on.

- Logging is a key layer for any kind of software container. Apache Karaf provides a powerful and very dynamic logging system powered by Pax Logging. In your OSGi application, you are not coupled to a specific logging framework; you can use the framework of your choice (slf4j, log4j, logback, commons-logging, and so on). Apache Karaf uses a central configuration file irrespective of the logging frameworks in use. All changes in this configuration file are made on the fly; no need to restart anything. Again, Apache Karaf provides commands and MBeans dedicated to log management (changing the log level, direct display of the log in the shell console, and so on).

- Hot deployment is also an interesting feature provided by Apache Karaf. By default, the container monitors a deploy folder periodically. When a new file is dropped in the deploy folder, Apache Karaf checks the file type and delegates the deployment logic for this file to a deployer. Apache Karaf provides different deployers by default (spring, blueprint, features, war, and so on).

- If **Java Authentication and Authorization Service (JAAS)** is the Java implementation of **Pluggable Authentication Modules (PAM)**, it's not very OSGi compliant by default. Apache Karaf leverages JAAS, exposing realm and login modules as OSGi services. Again, Apache Karaf provides dedicated JAAS shell commands and MBeans. The security framework is very flexible, allowing you to define the chain of login modules that you want for authentication. By default, Apache Karaf uses a `PropertiesLoginModule` using the `etc/users.properties` file for storage. The security framework also provides support for password encryption (you just have to enable encryption in the `etc/org.apache.karaf.jaas.cfg` configuration file). The new Apache Karaf version (3.0.0) also provides a complete **Role Based Access Control (RBAC)** system, allowing you to configure the users who can run commands, call MBeans, and so on.

- Apache Karaf is an enterprise-ready container and provides features dedicated to enterprise. The following enterprise features are not installed by default (to minimize the size and footprint of the container by default), but a simple command allows you to extend the container with enterprise functionalities:
    - WebContainer allows you to deploy a **Web Application Bundle (WAB)** or WAR file. Apache Karaf is a complete HTTP server with JSP/servlet support, thanks to Pax Web.
    - **Java Naming and Directory Interface (JNDI)** adds naming context support in Apache Karaf. You can bind an OSGi service to a JNDI name and look up these services using the name, thanks to Aries and Xbean naming.
    - **Java Transaction API (JTA)** allows you to add a transaction engine (exposed as an OSGi service) in Apache Karaf, thanks to Aries JTA.
    - **Java Persistence API (JPA)** allows you to add a persistence adapter (exposed as an OSGi service) in Apache Karaf, thanks to Aries JPA. Ready-to-use persistence engines can also be installed very easily (especially Apache OpenJPA and Hibernate).
    - **Java Database Connectivity (JDBC)** or **Java Message Service (JMS)** are convenient features, allowing you to easily create JDBC DataSources or JMS ConnectionFactories and use them directly in the shell console.

- If you can completely administrate Apache Karaf using the shell commands and the JMX MBeans, you can also install Web Console. This Web Console uses the Felix Web Console and allows you to manage Karaf with a simple browser.

Thanks to these features, Apache Karaf is a complete, rich, and enterprise-ready container. We can consider Apache Karaf as an OSGi application server.

Provisioning in Apache Karaf

In addition, Apache Karaf provides three core functionalities that can be used both internally in Apache Karaf or can be used by external applications deployed in the container:

- OSGi bundle management
- Configuration management
- Provisioning using Karaf Features

As we learned earlier, the default artifact in OSGi is the bundle. Again, it's a regular JAR file with additional OSGi metadata in the MANIFEST file. The bundles are directly managed by the OSGi framework, but for convenience, Apache Karaf wraps the usage of bundles in specific commands and MBeans.

A bundle has a specific life cycle. Especially when you install a bundle, the OSGi framework tries to resolve all the dependencies required by your bundle to promote it in a resolved state. The following is the life cycle of a bundle:

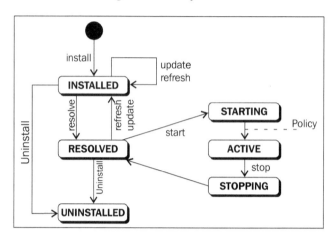

The OSGi framework checks whether other bundles provide the packages imported by your bundle. The equivalent action for the OSGi services is performed when you start your bundle. It means that a bundle may require a lot of other bundles to start and so on for the transitive bundles.

Moreover, a bundle may require configuration to work. Apache Karaf proposes a very convenient way to manage the configurations. The etc folder is periodically monitored to discover new configuration files and load the corresponding configurations. On the other hand, you have dedicated shell commands and MBeans to manage configurations (and configuration files). If a bundle requires a configuration to work, you first have to create a configuration file in the etc folder (with the expected filename) or use the config:* shell command or ConfigMBean to create the configuration.

Considering that an OSGi application is a set of bundles, the installation of an OSGi application can be long and painful by hand.

The deployment of an OSGi application is called provisioning as it gathers the following:

- The installation of a set of bundles, including transitive bundles
- The installation of a set of configurations required by these bundles

OBR

OSGi Bundle Repository (OBR) can be the first option to be considered in order to solve this problem. Apache Karaf can connect to the OBR server. The OBR server stores all the metadata for all the bundles, which includes the capabilities, packages, and services provided by a bundle and the requirements, packages, and services needed by a bundle. When you install a bundle via OBR, the OBR server checks the requirement of the installed bundle and finds the bundles that provide the capabilities matching the requirements. The OBR server can automatically install the bundles required for the first one.

Apache Karaf Features

As a lightweight and standalone OSGi container, Apache Karaf proposes another way to provision applications. Apache Karaf Features is the default provisioning solution in Apache Karaf.

Karaf Features describes an application, declaring the following aspects:

- The bundles in the application
- Other Karaf features required by the application
- Configurations required by the application

A Karaf Feature repository is a simple XML file describing a set of Karaf features. A Karaf Feature repository looks like the following:

```
<features name="my-features">

  <feature name="core-feature" version="1.0">
    <bundle>mvn:bundleA_groupId/bundleA_artifactId/bundleA_version
    </bundle>
    <bundle>file:/path/to/bundleB</bundle>
    <bundle>http://path/to/bundleC</bundle>
  </feature>

  <feature name="extend-feature" version="1.0">
    <feature version="[1,2)">core-feature</feature>
```

```
        <bundle>mvn:bundleD_groupId/bundleD_artifactId/bundleD_version
        </bundle>
    <config name="my.configuration.pid">
        key1=value1
       key2=value2
    </config>
  </feature>

  <feature name="other-feature" version="1.1">
    <feature version="[1,2)">core-feature</feature>
    <bundle>mvn:bundleE_groupId/bundleE_artifactId/bundleE_version
    </bundle>
    <configfile finalname="/etc/my.configuration.cfg">
    http://path/to/file/my.cfg
    </configfile>
  </feature>

</features>
```

Note that Apache Karaf supports different types of URLs, as follows:

- A file URL allows you to install a bundle or a configuration file located in the local filesystem.

- An HTTP URL allows you to download and install a bundle or a configuration file located on an HTTP server.

- An Mvn URL allows you to directly use Maven repositories. The URL uses the Maven information (`groupId/artifactId/version/classifier/type`) and converts this URL to an HTTP URL relative to different repositories (described in `etc/org.ops4j.pax.url.mvn.cfg`).

This gives us a very flexible way to get the artifacts required for the application. The artifacts can be local or remote, on a pure HTTP server or on a Maven repository manager (such as Apache Archiva, Nexus, or even Maven Central).

Karaf Features completely describes applications and eventually dependencies between applications and the required configuration. In our example, we can note the following:

- The core-feature feature installs bundle A, bundle B, and bundle C using different protocols: local filesystem for bundle A, downloading from an HTTP server for bundle B, and using Maven for bundle C (from a Maven repository).

- The extend-feature feature requires core-feature. This means that if core-feature is not already installed, Apache Karaf will install it first. Once core-feature is installed, bundle D will be installed (and started) from a Maven repository. This feature also creates a configuration with the `my.configuration.pid` ID and populates this configuration with the key-value pairs directly defined in the element.

- The other-feature feature also requires core-feature (as for extend-feature, core-feature will be installed if it's not already the case). Bundle E will be installed and started using Maven (from a Maven repository). The other-feature feature will also create a configuration, but this time using a base configuration file installed in the `etc` folder of Apache Karaf. The configuration file is downloaded using one URL supported by Apache Karaf (in this example, an HTTP URL is used).

Thanks to Karaf Features, provisioning is pretty easy and straightforward.

The first action consists of registering the Karaf Features repository in the container using the `features:addurl` shell command (or the corresponding operation on FeaturesMBean). Once done, you can see the list of Karaf features available using the `features:list` command.

To install an OSGi application, just install the corresponding Karaf feature with `features:install`.

Multiple Apache Karaf containers

Natively, Apache Karaf provides a high availability mechanism based on a locking system. It's a master-slaves configuration, following an active/passive pattern. Apache Karaf supports two kinds of locks, which are as follows:

- Lock on the filesystem
- Lock on a database (JDBC)

When the first Apache Karaf instance starts, if the lock is available, the instance acquires the lock and becomes the master.

If another instance starts, as the lock is not available (held by the master), the instance is in standby (slave) mode and periodically checks the lock.

When you use a lock on a filesystem, all instances have to share the same filesystem. The lock is a simple file. If the Apache Karaf instances are located on different machines, it means that the filesystem storing the lock has to be available for all machines (using NFS, CIFS, SAN, and so on).

In order to enable the filesystem locking system, you have to update the etc/system.properties configuration file as follows:

```
karaf.lock=true
karaf.lock.class=org.apache.karaf.main.SimpleFileLock
karaf.lock.dir=/path/to/lockfile
karaf.lock.delay=10
```

When a shared filesystem is not an option (for security or infrastructure reasons, for instance), you can use a database to store the lock. With database locking, Apache Karaf uses a lock on a table (the KARAF_LOCK table by default). Any database that supports JDBC can be used.

The configuration is also defined in the etc/system.properties configuration file as follows:

```
karaf.lock=true
karaf.lock.class=org.apache.karaf.main.DefaultJDBCLock
karaf.lock.level=50
karaf.lock.delay=10
karaf.lock.jdbc.url=jdbc:derby://dbserver:1527/sample
karaf.lock.jdbc.driver=org.apache.derby.jdbc.ClientDriver
karaf.lock.jdbc.user=user
karaf.lock.jdbc.password=password
karaf.lock.jdbc.table=KARAF_LOCK
karaf.lock.jdbc.clustername=karaf
karaf.lock.jdbc.timeout=30
```

You have to copy the JDBC driver JAR file into the lib/ext folder. Apache Karaf provides the JDBC lock implementation dedicated to some specific databases (DefaultJDBCLock is the generic one, OracleJDBCLock for Oracle databases, DerbyJDBCLock for Derby databases, MySQLJDBCLock for MySQL databases, PostgreSQLJDBCLock for PostgreSQL databases, and SQLServerJDBCLock for Microsoft SQLServer databases).

The Apache Karaf locking mechanism provides a good solution for high availability. However, only one Apache Karaf instance is active (the master); all other instances are inactive (standby/master).

In order to provide both high availability and performance scalability, having multiple active Apache Karaf instances is a great advantage.

Provisioning clusters

Imagine you have a farm of Apache Karaf containers, each on a different machine. If you want to provision an OSGi application on the container instances, you have to connect on each container and install the features.

This means that you have to perform the following tasks:

- Log on on each container in order to perform the same action again and again
- Eventually, adapt the configuration depending on each local instance (port number, file path, and so on)
- Add new instances, which will require the same action again

Basically, this means a lot of human actions with a potential risk of error. This is where a provisioning cluster helps.

The purpose of a provisioning cluster is to keep multiple container instances synchronized. For Apache Karaf, it means that a change in the status of a resource will be broadcasted to all the containers' members of the same cluster.

A resource can be a bundle, feature, configuration, or any kind of resource local to a node. This means that local actions will send an event to update the other members of the cluster.

On the other hand, it's also possible to create a cluster event that is sent to all the members to update them.

Basically, this means that a provisioning cluster performs the following tasks:

- **Creates event**: This event can be created due to a local change or by hand
- **Broadcasts event**: This event is sent to the members of the cluster

If provisioning is the first purpose of a provisioning cluster, it doesn't mean that it can't provide additional features useful in a cluster topology. For instance, centralized logs, load balancers, session replication, and so on are interesting features that can be provided on top of a provisioning cluster. In the next chapters, we will see Karaf Cellar as a provisioning cluster solution.

Summary

In this chapter, we reviewed the goals of OSGi and some core components (bundles, manifests, and so on). We also quickly introduced the Apache Karaf OSGi container, describing the different provided features. Finally, we dealt with the different ways to use multiple Apache Karaf instances altogether: an active/passive way (failover) or active/active way (provisioning cluster).

The next chapter will introduce the Apache Karaf Cellar provisioning cluster.

Apache Karaf Cellar

_2_

Apache Karaf Cellar is a provisioning cluster solution for Apache Karaf.

It's an Apache Karaf subproject released under the Apache 2 license. To know more, please visit `http://karaf.apache.org/index/subprojects/cellar.html`.

Apache Karaf Cellar allows you to manage a farm of Apache Karaf instances spread over different machines and networks.

As a provisioning cluster solution, Apache Karaf Cellar synchronizes the states of the different instances. By synchronization, we mean that an action on a resource from a node will result in a notification to change for the other nodes.

The following topics will be covered in this chapter:

- Cluster topologies
- Apache Karaf Cellar architecture
- Apache Karaf Cellar installation
- Cluster resources

Cluster topologies

When we talk about provisioning clusters, it means that we have to store and share the status of resources between different instances.

We name the node as an instance member of the provisioning cluster.

We can see two approaches to share the status of the resources.

The first approach is to use a central component to store the status. This central component is named `cluster manager`. It's responsible for storing the data shared between the nodes and the communication between the nodes. Have a look at the following diagram:

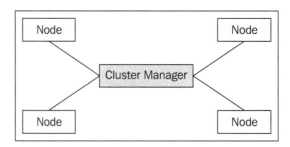

All nodes are connected to a central component storing the status of the resources. For instance, this component could be Apache ZooKeeper.

The advantage of this approach is that the provisioning cluster has no impact on the nodes; a node just communicates with the central component.

The cluster manager is not just a simple shared storage, as it has to deal with the communication and transport of information between the nodes.

A drawback of this approach is that the cluster manager is a single point of failure.

In order to guarantee a reliable cluster and high availability, the cluster manager itself should be clustered: we have to provide and install a farm of cluster managers.

This means that you have two layers of clustering, as follows:

- The actual cluster between the nodes
- The **Cluster Manager** cluster just to guarantee high availability

In Apache Karaf Cellar, a different approach has been chosen. The following diagram will give you a brief idea of this approach:

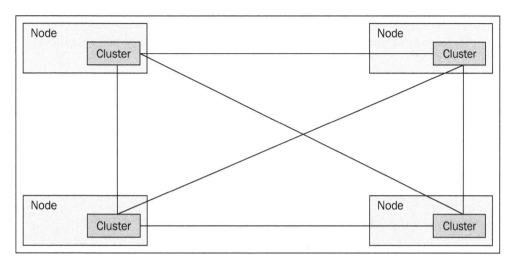

Each node embeds its own cluster component, which communicates with the other nodes.

The purposes of the cluster component are as follows:

- It is a local representation of the resource's status of the cluster. The resource's status is replicated and distributed on every cluster component.
- It manages the discovery and visibility of the nodes and transports information from one node to the others. It's a **cluster event** model.

This means that changing the status of a resource will trigger two actions, and they are:

- The distributed status is updated. This means that the cluster component on each node is updated.
- The cluster component from the node sends an event to the other nodes, informing them that a resource has changed and they need to update their local status.

Thanks to this approach, Apache Karaf Cellar provides the following:

- It is a very reliable solution. We just need one node active to have a valid cluster. The cluster is fault-tolerant by itself.

- A distributed status on the cluster with a cluster event synchronization mechanism.

Apache Karaf Cellar architecture

Apache Karaf Cellar provides an API to implement the cluster component. The default cluster component implementation is powered by **Hazelcast**.

Hazelcast is a clustering and scalable data distribution solution. It provides features that exactly match the needs for the cluster component, especially the following:

- A distributed storage implementation. This is where Apache Karaf Cellar will store the resources' status.

- A distributed topic for publish/subscribe messaging. Apache Karaf Cellar will use this distributed topic to implement cluster events.

These are the two functionalities we are looking for in our cluster component.

However, Hazelcast also provides additional features. Thanks to Hazelcast, Apache Karaf Cellar supports different ways to discover the nodes of the cluster: static IP address definition, multicast, and whiteboard registration. The following diagram shows the modules provided by Karaf:

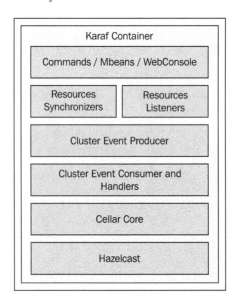

The first thing to do is install Cellar in the different Karaf containers that have been targeted to be members of the cluster (the nodes).

As Apache Karaf Cellar is packaged as a Karaf Feature, we have to install the Cellar feature. This means that Cellar is a set of bundles and configuration files.

Installing the Apache Karaf Cellar feature provides the following modules:

- **Hazelcast**: Apache Karaf Cellar directly leverages Hazelcast, and just wraps some features (such as node discovery).

- **Cellar core**: By default, Cellar works with Hazelcast. However, it's possible to change the implementation (for instance, it is possible to replace Hazelcast with Apache ZooKeeper, Apache ActiveMQ, or a custom implementation). The Cellar Core module provides the API used by the other modules. Cellar Core delegates API usage to the actual implementation. Most importantly, the API provides operations to manipulate the resource's status storage on the cluster.

- **Cluster event producer**: This module is part of the messaging layer. The producer is responsible for creating a cluster event and broadcasting this event to the other nodes. The producer actually creates a message (the cluster event) and sends it to a Hazelcast distributed topic.

- **Cluster event consumer and handlers**: On the other hand, the cluster event is received by the cluster event consumer. The cluster event consumer is actually a subscriber on the Hazelcast distributed topic. Thanks to the cluster event producer and consumer, we have a very dynamic system: when a new node joins the cluster, its cluster event consumer subscribes to the topic. We have a plug-and-play solution. However, the cluster event consumer doesn't handle the cluster event itself. It delegates the event processing to a cluster event handler. We have one cluster event handler per kind of resource. Thanks to this approach, it's possible to easily add new resources managed in the cluster. The cluster event producer and consumer are generic; the cluster event handlers are dedicated to the resource management.

- **Resources synchronizers**: This module is responsible for the synchronization of a resource local to a node, with the status of this resource on the cluster. The synchronizer is called when installing Apache Karaf Cellar and when the node joins the cluster.

- **Resources listeners**: This module listens for local resource changes, creates cluster events, and sends them to the other nodes in the cluster.

- **Commands, MBeans, WebConsole plugin**: These modules interact with the cluster, check the status of the nodes, check the status of the resources, and so on. Apache Karaf Cellar provides a set of shell commands and operations on MBean. An optional feature also provides a WebConsole plugin, which extends the Apache Karaf WebConsole with cluster views.

Apache Karaf Cellar installation and first commands

Apache Karaf Cellar is provided as a Karaf feature.

Throughout this book, we will use the following installation:

- Node 1 is a server running with the 192.168.1.1 network address. It hosts an Apache Karaf 2.3.3 instance running in the /opt/apache-karaf folder.
- Node 2 is another server running with the 192.168.1.2 network address. It hosts an Apache Karaf 2.3.3 instance running in the /opt/apache-karaf folder.
- Both servers have Internet access.

We connect to the Apache Karaf instance on node 1 (using SSH or client) to install the Apache Karaf Cellar feature, as follows:

```
karaf@node1> features:addurl mvn:org.apache.karaf.cellar/apache-
   karaf-cellar/2.3.1/xml/features
karaf@node1> features:install cellar
```

It's done! Apache Karaf Cellar is installed and operating on node1.

We can now install Apache Karaf Cellar on node 2. We connect on node 2 (using SSH or client) and install the Apache Karaf Cellar feature, as follows:

```
karaf@node2> features:addurl mvn:org.apache.karaf.cellar/apache-
   karaf-cellar/2.3.1/xml/features
karaf@node2> features:install cellar
```

We now have new shell commands dedicated to the cluster. For instance, it's possible to see the nodes in the cluster using the cluster:node-list command, as follows:

```
karaf@node1> cluster:node-list
     ID                       Host Name        Port
   [192.168.1.2:5702   ]    [192.168.1.2]    [ 5702]
 * [192.168.1.1:5701   ]    [192.168.1.1]    [ 5701]
```

We can now see our two servers. The * indicates the local node (where we are connected and will execute commands from).

It's also possible to test the network between different nodes using the
`cluster:node-ping` command as follows:

```
karaf@node1> cluster:node-ping 192.168.1.2:5702
PING 192.168.1.2:5702
from 1: req=192.168.1.2:5702 time=57 ms
from 2: req=192.168.1.2:5702 time=17 ms
from 3: req=192.168.1.2:5702 time=20 ms
from 4: req=192.168.1.2:5702 time=23 ms
from 5: req=192.168.1.2:5702 time=22 ms
from 6: req=192.168.1.2:5702 time=17 ms
from 7: req=192.168.1.2:5702 time=20 ms
```

Cluster resources

By default, Apache Karaf Cellar supports the clustering and distribution of
different resources.

Cellar is able to manage the resources covered in the following sections.

Bundles

Apache Karaf Cellar is able to sync the status of OSGi bundles on the cluster.

Thanks to the bundle listener, all actions that you may perform on a bundle are
spread onto the cluster. You can also use dedicated cluster commands to manipulate
the bundles on the cluster.

For instance, it's possible to see the bundles available on the cluster with their current
status using the `cluster:bundle-list` command as follows:

```
karaf@node1> cluster:bundle-list default
Bundles in cluster group default
  ID      State      Name
[0    ] [Active] Apache Karaf :: Cellar :: Utils (2.3.1)
[1    ] [Active] Apache Karaf :: JAAS :: Config (2.3.3)
[2    ] [Active] Apache Karaf :: Diagnostic :: Command (2.3.3)
[3    ] [Active] Apache Karaf :: Deployer :: Spring (2.3.3)
[4    ] [Active] Apache Aries Proxy Service (1.0.1)
[5    ] [Active] Apache Karaf :: Management :: MBeans :: Dev (2.3.3)
```

```
[6   ] [Active] Apache Karaf :: Management :: MBeans :: System
(2.3.3)
[7   ] [Active] Apache Aries Blueprint Core (1.1.0)
[8   ] [Active] Apache Karaf :: Shell :: Development Commands (2.3.3)
[9   ] [Active] Apache Karaf :: Features :: Command (2.3.3)
[10  ] [Active] Apache Karaf :: Diagnostic :: Common (2.3.3)
[11  ] [Active] Apache Karaf :: Admin :: Management (2.3.3)
```

The default argument is the Cellar cluster group. Cellar uses a default cluster group named `default`. We will see more details about cluster groups in another chapter of this book.

We can install a bundle on the cluster using the `cluster:bundle-install` command.

For instance, we install the `commons-lang` bundle on the cluster (from node 1) as follows:

```
karaf@node1> cluster:bundle-install default mvn:commons-lang/
commons-lang/2.6
```

This command creates and sends a cluster event to all nodes (including the local one) to install the `commons-lang` bundle. Now, if we check the `commons-lang` bundle status on the cluster using the following code, we can see that it's installed:

```
karaf@node1> cluster:bundle-list -l default|grep -i commons-lang

[60  ] [Installed ] mvn:commons-lang/commons-lang/2.6
```

> The -l option displays the location of the bundles instead of their name.

We can check on node 1 and node 2 that the `commons-lang` bundle is installed locally to each node, as follows:

```
karaf@node1> la -l|grep -i commons-lang

[  63] [Installed ] [         ] [   80] mvn:commons-lang/
commons-lang/2.6


karaf@node2> la -l|grep -i commons-lang

[  63] [Installed ] [         ] [   80] mvn:commons-lang/
commons-lang/2.6
```

Our two nodes are in sync. The `commons-lang` bundle has been installed on both.

Now, we are going to start the `commons-lang` bundle. But, this time, instead of using the `cluster:bundle-start` command, we use the local `osgi:start` command on node 1. As we just installed the bundle, the bundle is not yet started. That's why we have to start the bundle now. Run the following command:

```
karaf@node1> osgi:start 63
```

Now, running the following command, we can see the `commons-lang` bundle started on node 1:

```
karaf@node1> la -l|grep -i commons-lang
[  63] [Active ] [            ] [   80] mvn:commons-lang/commons-lang/2.6
```

Thanks to the Cellar bundle listener, this local change has been caught by Cellar and broadcasted to the other nodes. So, this means that the `commons-lang` bundle should now be started on node 2 as well. Run the following command:

```
karaf@node2> la -l|grep -i commons-lang
[  63] [Active ] [            ] [   80] mvn:commons-lang/
commons-lang/2.6
```

Here we are again, and our two nodes are still in sync.

To summarize, Apache Karaf Cellar supports all actions that you may perform on a bundle (install, start, stop, uninstall, refresh, and so on).

By default, all local actions are spread to the cluster thanks to the Cellar bundle listeners.

You can also use dedicated `cluster:bundle-*` commands.

In addition to the `cluster:bundle-*` commands, you can also use the Cellar BundleMBean over JMX. This MBean allows you to manipulate the bundles on the cluster with any kind of JMX client (such as JConsole), as shown in the following screenshot:

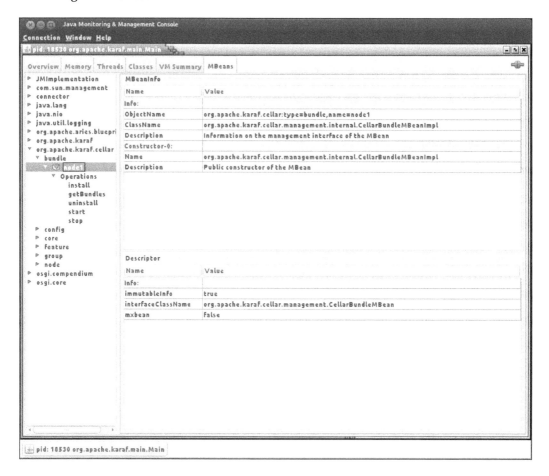

Karaf features

Apache Karaf Cellar is also able to sync Karaf features.

The Cellar features listener spreads all local actions to a feature on the cluster, just as for a bundle.

You also have the `cluster:feature-*` shell commands to manipulate the Karaf features on the cluster.

For instance, it's possible to see the Karaf Features repository URLs on the cluster with the help of the following commands:

```
karaf@node1> cluster:feature-url-list default
mvn:org.apache.karaf.cellar/apache-karaf-cellar/2.3.1/xml/features
mvn:org.jclouds.karaf/jclouds-karaf/1.4.0/xml/features
mvn:org.apache.karaf.assemblies.features/enterprise/2.3.3/xml/
features
mvn:org.apache.karaf.assemblies.features/standard/2.3.3/xml/
features
```

The status of the features can be checked using the following commands:

```
karaf@node1> cluster:feature-list default|more
Features in cluster group default
 Status        Version        Name
[uninstalled] [3.0.7.RELEASE ] spring
[uninstalled] [2.3.1         ] cellar-eventadmin
[uninstalled] [2.3.3         ] scr
[uninstalled] [1.4.0         ] jclouds-cloudfiles-uk
[uninstalled] [1.4.0         ] jclouds-services
[uninstalled] [1.4.0         ] jclouds-aws-s3
[uninstalled] [1.4.0         ] jclouds-cloudserver-us
```

Note that we can see the local status and cluster status of the eventadmin feature as follows:

```
karaf@node1> features:list|grep -i eventadmin
[uninstalled] [2.3.3         ] eventadmin
  karaf-2.3.3         OSGi Event Admin service specification for event-
based communication
karaf@node1> cluster:feature-list default|grep -i eventadmin
[uninstalled] [2.3.3         ] eventadmin
```

Now we want to install the eventadmin feature on the cluster using the cluster:feature-install command. We shall do so with the following command:

```
karaf@node1> cluster:feature-install default eventadmin
```

We can check the status of the eventadmin feature on the cluster as follows:

```
karaf@node1> cluster:feature-list default|grep -i eventadmin
[installed  ] [2.3.3         ] eventadmin
```

We can now see that the eventadmin feature is installed. Let's check whether this is the case locally on node 1 and node 2 with the following commands:

```
karaf@node1> features:list|grep -i eventadmin

[installed  ] [2.3.3      ] eventadmin                        karaf-2.3.3
OSGi Event Admin service specification for event-based communication


karaf@node2> features:list|grep -i eventadmin

[installed  ] [2.3.3      ] eventadmin                        karaf-2.3.3
OSGi Event Admin service specification for event-based communication
```

Our two nodes are in sync and the eventadmin feature is installed on both.

Now we want to uninstall the eventadmin feature, but instead of using the dedicated cluster:feature-uninstall command, we use the local features:uninstall command on node 1, as follows:

```
karaf@node1> features:uninstall eventadmin
```

Thanks to the Cellar features listener, this local change is spread across the cluster. We can check the status of the eventadmin feature on the cluster, as follows:

```
karaf@node1> cluster:feature-list default|grep -i eventadmin

[uninstalled] [2.3.3      ] eventadmin
```

And locally on node 2 as follows:

```
karaf@node2> features:list|grep -i eventadmin

[uninstalled] [2.3.3      ] eventadmin
karaf-2.3.3        OSGi Event Admin service specification for event-based
communication
```

As we can see, node 1 and 2 are still in sync. Apache Karaf Cellar provides a Cellar FeatureMBean, allowing you to perform cluster operations with any kind of JMX client (such as JConsole), just as for a bundle, as shown in the following screenshot:

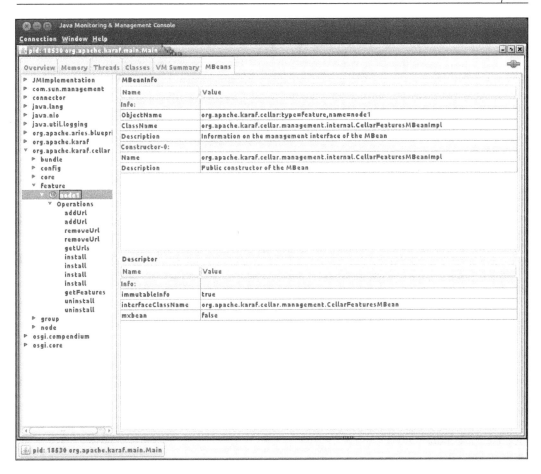

Configuration

In addition to bundles and features, Apache Karaf Cellar also supports the synchronization and distribution of configurations.

You can see the list of configurations on the cluster using the `cluster:config-list` command as follows:

```
karaf@node1> cluster:config-list default

-----------------------------------------------------------------
Pid:         org.apache.karaf.features.repos
Properties:
   service.pid = org.apache.karaf.features.repos
   openejb = org.apache.openejb:openejb-feature:xml:features:(0,]
```

```
jclouds = org.jclouds.karaf:jclouds-karaf:xml:features:(0,]
camel = org.apache.camel.karaf:apache-camel:xml:features:(0,]
cxf-dosgi = org.apache.cxf.dosgi:cxf-dosgi:xml:features:(0,]
wicket = org.ops4j.pax.wicket:features:xml:features:(0,]
```

We create the my configuration containing the key property by using the following command line:

```
karaf@node1> cluster:config-propset default my key value
```

And see the configuration on the cluster using the following command:

```
karaf@node1> cluster:config-list default

...

Pid:        my
Properties:
   key = value
   service.pid = my
```

We can check if this configuration has been created by Cellar locally to node 1 and 2 by using the following command:

```
karaf@node1> config:list "(service.pid=my)"
----------------------------------------------------------------
Pid:        my
BundleLocation: null
Properties:
   service.pid = my
   key = value


karaf@node2> config:list "(service.pid=my)"
----------------------------------------------------------------
Pid:        my
BundleLocation: null
Properties:
   service.pid = my
   key = value
```

Again, both the nodes are in sync. The my configuration has been replicated on nodes 1 and 2.

Now we want to change the value to other for the key property. But instead of using the cluster:config-propset command, we are directly using the local Karaf native config:* commands on node 1 as follows:

```
karaf@node1> config:edit my
karaf@node1> config:propset key other
karaf@node1> config:update
```

Thanks to the Cellar Configuration listener, the status of the my configuration has been updated on the cluster:

```
karaf@node1> cluster:config-list default
...
Pid:          my
Properties:
   key = other
   service.pid = my
We can check that "my"configuration has been updated on node2 as well:

karaf@node2> config:list "(service.pid=my)"
----------------------------------------------------------------
Pid:          my
BundleLocation: null
Properties:
   service.pid = my
   key = other
```

Again, both the nodes are in sync.

Apache Karaf Cellar provides a Cellar ConfigMBean, allowing you to manipulate the cluster with any kind of JMX clients (such as JConsole), just as for bundles and features, as shown in the following screenshot:

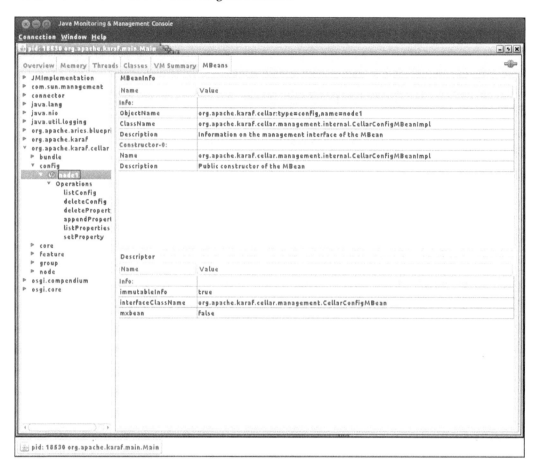

Optional resources

In addition to the default bundles, features, and configurations' resources support, Apache Karaf Cellar provides some optional resources support.

To enable the support of these resources, you have to install the following dedicated Cellar features:

- The `cellar-eventadmin` feature that adds cluster support to the `eventadmin` feature. This means that all local OSGi events on a node are broadcasted to the other nodes.

- The `cellar-obr` feature that adds cluster support to the OBR service. This means that the OBR repositories' URLs are distributed to all nodes in the cluster. You can also use dedicated shell commands (and MBean operations) to install bundles using the OBR service.

The Karaf WebConsole plugin

Optionally, you can install the `cellar-webconsole` feature. This feature installs and registers a plugin to the Karaf WebConsole, displaying the available Cellar cluster groups. When installing the `WebConsole` feature, Karaf provides a URL (by default, the URL is `http://localhost:8181/system/console`) where you can manage the container using a simple browser. The `webconsole` feature is secured using a login and password (`karaf/karaf` by default). The `cellar-webconsole` feature adds new pages in this `webconsole`. The following command will install the `cellar-webconsole` feature:

```
karaf@node1> features:install cellar-webconsole
```

The following screenshot is how the Karaf WebConsole will look:

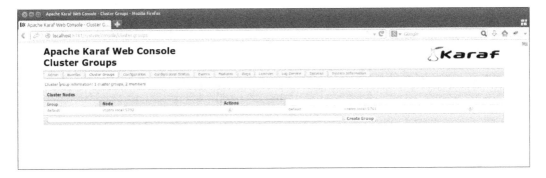

Summary

In this chapter, we have introduced the Apache Karaf Cellar topology and architecture.

We also installed Apache Karaf Cellar and used some basic commands to sync two nodes in a cluster. The next chapter will describe the configuration files used by Apache Karaf Cellar and the usage of Hazelcast.

3
Hazelcast

Hazelcast is the heart of Cellar and is used in the core module. The Cellar core module specifies the cluster behavior but does not specify the implementation. The default Cellar implementation is powered by Hazelcast. Cellar directly leverages the Hazelcast features to provide the functionalities expected in the cluster, such as discovering the cluster nodes, communication between the nodes, and distributing the states of the resources in the cluster.

In this chapter, we will deal with the following topics:

- An introduction to Hazelcast and its features
- An understanding of how Cellar uses Hazelcast
- Creating a custom extension to Hazelcast

What is Hazelcast?

Hazelcast is a cluster and distribution solution. In Cellar, each node embeds a Hazelcast instance. The Hazelcast instances can identify each other using different mechanisms. Once connected, these Hazelcast instances share a state and distribute objects in the cluster, which are listed as follows:

- A distributed form of set and map, allowing Cellar to store the status of the resources in the cluster.
- A distributed topic and queue used by Cellar to transport the cluster events from a node to the other nodes. It's similar to the topic and queue destinations that we find in messaging systems such as JMS—a node can act as a producer/consumer on a queue and/or as a publisher/subscriber on a topic.
- Multiple network configurations and discovery mechanisms, allowing Cellar nodes to automatically discover and see the other nodes.

Cellar wraps the Hazelcast instance in an OSGi way; this means that the Hazelcast instance is exposed as an OSGi service and can be used by any client bundle. For communication between the nodes, Cellar uses the Hazelcast TCP/IP layer with Java NIO.

Cellar automatically installs a Hazelcast configuration file in `etc/hazelcast.xml`. The Hazelcast configuration and tuning is stored in this file. This chapter covers the contents of this configuration file.

Distributed cluster resource states

Cellar uses Hazelcast to maintain and store the states of the different resources in the cluster (bundles, features, configuration, OBR, eventadmin, DOSGi, and so on). To do so, Cellar uses Hazelcast's distributed data structures. Thanks to this, the cluster data is distributed across all the nodes in the cluster. Each Cellar node stores a portion of the data (and eventually the replicas/backups).

For instance, in Cellar, you have the following three features installed:

- Feature A
- Feature B
- Feature C

The statuses of the features are stored in a distributed map that looks similar to the following statuses:

- Feature A: Installed
- Feature B: Uninstalled
- Feature C: Installed

The partition of the features' distributed map (in the cluster) can be as follows:

- Feature A's status on node1
- Feature B's status on node2
- Feature C's status on node1

If a node goes down or leaves the cluster, Hazelcast redistributes the data (including the replica) on the remaining nodes. Similarly, when a new node joins the cluster, Hazelcast redispatches the data on the different nodes.

Thus, there is no cluster manager or a single point of failure: each node in the cluster acts the same as the next.

Distributed queues and topics

Cellar uses distributed queues and topics for communication between nodes.

When a resource changes on a node (for instance, you install a new feature on this node), Cellar creates a cluster event and sends it into a queue or a topic (depending on whether the cluster event is targeted towards one node or is global).

On the other hand, the other nodes can consume this cluster event and react accordingly (they will install the feature locally).

A Hazelcast distributed queue is an implementation of `java.util.concurrent.BlockingQueue`. As a regular queue, the elements in the queue are ordered in the FIFO mode. Again, as this queue is distributed across the Cellar nodes, the elements in the queue are objects that implement `java.io.Serializable`. By default, there is no limit to the number of elements in the queue and the **time to live** (**TTL**) of these elements. Now, if you have a bad connection between the cluster nodes (network issues or different WAN/datacenters), you may have a very high number of elements in the queue (you enqueue faster than you dequeue). In that case, a good practice is to define a limit for the queues in `etc/hazelcast.xml`.

The maximum capacity per Cellar instance and the TTL for a queue can be configured in the `etc/hazelcast.xml` file. For instance, we can limit the size of the queue using the `max-size-per-jvm` element to define a custom storage for the queue using the `map-store` element, as shown in the following code:

```
<hazelcast>
    ...
    <queue name="*">
        <!-- Maximum size of the queue. When a JVM's local queue
            size reaches the maximum, all put/offer operations will
            get blocked until the queue size of the JVM goes down
            below the maximum. Any integer between 0 and
            Integer.MAX_VALUE. 0 means Integer.MAX_VALUE.
            Default is 0. -->
        <max-size-per-jvm>10000</max-size-per-jvm>
        <!-- Name of the map configuration that will be used for
            the backing distributed map for this queue. -->
        <backing-map-ref>queue-map</backing-map-ref>
    </queue>
    <map name="queue-map">
        <backup-count>1</backup-count>
        <map-store enabled="true">
            <class-name>org.example.MyStore</class-name>
            <write-delay-seconds>0</write-delay-seconds>
        </map-store>
        ...
    </map>
</hazelcast>
```

By default, Cellar stores the resource status in an in-memory distributed queue (without the `map-store` configuration). You can provide a store implementation to persist the queue in a backend such as a database for instance.

The Cellar distributed map

Cellar uses a distributed map to store the statuses of the resources in the cluster. For this, the following are the instances:

- The list and current statuses of the features in the cluster are stored in a distributed map that looks as follows:
    - Feature A: Installed
    - Feature B: Uninstalled

- The list and current statuses of the bundles in the cluster are stored in a distributed map that looks as follows:
    - Bundle A: Installed
    - Bundle B: Started
    - Bundle C: Uninstalled

- The list of configurations and properties on the cluster are stored in a distributed map that looks as follows:
    - PID A: Properties
    - PID B: Properties

These map entries are partitioned on the cluster nodes. This means that each node has a piece of the map.

Replicas/Backup

By default, distributed maps have one replica to insure failover; when an entry is added or updated in the map, Hazelcast synchronously creates a replica on another node.

Hazelcast manages the replicas with a backup operation; it provides the following two kinds of operations:

- Sync backup operations
- Async backup operations

Cellar only uses a sync backup operation to ensure that the replica is complete before it moves forward. You can increase the number of replicas using the `backup-count` element in the `etc/hazelcast.xml` file.

By default, the replicas are used only when a node goes down; Hazelcast can reload the data located on the failed node using the replica present on another node.

However, in a real runtime environment, a node has to call the node that stores the data, even if it holds a replica of this data locally.

To increase the read performance, you can allow the nodes to read their local replicas instead of actually calling the nodes that store the data. To do this, you just have to enable `read-backup-data` in the `etc/hazelcast.xml` file:

```
<hazelcast>
    ...
    <map name="*">
        <!-- Number of sync-backups. If 1 is set as the backup-
            count for example, then all entries of the map will be
            copied to another JVM for fail-safety.
            Valid numbers are 0 (no backup), 1, 2, 3. -->
        <backup-count>1</backup-count>
        <!-- Can we read the local backup entries? Default value
            is false for strong consistency. Being able to read
            backup data will give you greater performance. -->
        <read-backup-data>false</read-backup-data>
        ...
    </map>
</hazelcast>
```

Persistence

As we have seen in the previous section, Cellar uses an in-memory distributed map by default. It's not a big deal as each node reconstructs the data at startup. However, for performance reasons and for the security of the data, you can implement a persistent data store for the maps used by Cellar, describing the persistent data store in the `etc/hazelcast.xml` file with the following code:

```
<hazelcast>
    ...
    <map name="*">
        ...
        <map-store enabled="true">
```

```
<!-- Name of the class implementing MapLoader and/or
  MapStore. The class should implement at least of
  these interfaces and contain no-argument
  constructor. Note that the inner classes are not
  supported. -->
<class-name>com.hazelcast.examples.DummyStore
</class-name>
<!-- Number of seconds to delay to call the
  MapStore.store(key, value). If the value is zero
  then it is write-through so
  MapStore.store(key, value) will be called as soon as
  the entry is updated. Otherwise it is write-behind
  so updates will be stored after write-delay-seconds
  value by calling Hazelcast.storeAll(map).
  Default value is 0. -->
<write-delay-seconds>0</write-delay-seconds>
          </map-store>
        </map>
    </hazelcast>
```

Networks

In the previous sections, we saw the Hazelcast resources used by Cellar to format and transport cluster events. The transport relays to the network (the wire). Hazelcast provides the configuration of the network that we can leverage in Cellar. In this section, we will see how to configure Cellar node discovery, how to secure the communication between the nodes, and how to support IPv6.

Multiple clusters

On the same network, you may want to define multiple Cellar clusters, especially when you use node discovery. A Cellar cluster is identified by a name and password in the etc/hazelcast.xml configuration file. You can separate your clusters in a simple way (for instance, per environment) using the following code:

```
<hazelcast>
    <group>
        <name>dev</name>
        <password>dev-pass</password>
    </group>
    ...
</hazelcast>
```

TCP/IP

If multicasting (which is the default) is not the preferred way of discovering the nodes, then you can configure a full TCP/IP cluster (also known as a static definition of the Cellar nodes).

In the following `etc/hazelcast.xml` file, we will disable multicast and prefer the `tcp-ip` discovery.

For this, we need to provide the list of hostnames or IP addresses of the machines hosting the different nodes:

```
<hazelcast>
    ...
    <network>
        <port auto-increment="true">5701</port>
        <join>
            <multicast enabled="false">
                <multicast-group>224.2.2.3</multicast-group>
                <multicast-port>54327</multicast-port>
            </multicast>
            <tcp-ip enabled="true">
                <hostname>machine1</hostname>
                <hostname>machine2</hostname>
                <hostname>machine3:5799</hostname>
                <interface>192.168.1.0-7</interface>
                <interface>192.168.1.21</interface>
            </tcp-ip>
        </join>
        ...
    </network>
    ...
</hazelcast>
```

Interfaces

By default, Cellar uses any network interface of the machine (`0.0.0.0`). However, on a server machine, it's classic to have multiple network interfaces. In that case, you can specify the interfaces that you want to use for Cellar; this can be done with the following code:

```
<hazelcast>
    ...
    <network>
        ....
        <interfaces enabled="true">
```

```
                    <interface>10.3.16.*</interface>
                    <interface>10.3.10.4-18</interface>
                    <interface>192.168.1.3</interface>
                </interfaces>
            </network>
            ...
    </hazelcast>
```

The configuration allows the usage of the * and – characters.

The * character indicates all the IP addresses on the netmask; in our example, `10.3.16.*` means `10.3.16.1`, `10.3.16.2`, `10.3.16.3`, and so on.

The – character indicates an IP address range; in our example, `10.3.10.4-18` means `10.3.10.4`, `10.3.10.5`, `10.3.10.6`, and so on up to `10.3.10.18`.

SSL

Cellar allows you to use SSL socket communication between all the Cellar members.

With SSL, the communication channels between the nodes are secure.

In `etc/hazelcast.xml`, you just have to enable `ssl` and provide the keystore that contains the SSL certificate, as shown in the following code:

```
    <hazelcast>
        ...
        <network>
            ...
            <ssl enabled="true">
                <factory-class-name>
                  com.hazelcast.nio.ssl.BasicSSLContextFactory
                </factory-class-name>
                <properties>
                    <property name="keyStore">keyStore</property>
                    <property name="keyStorePassword">
                        keyStorePassword</property>
                </properties>
            </ssl>
        </network>
        ...
    </hazelcast>
```

You have to provide an `SSLFactory` class. Hazelcast provides a `BasicSSLContextFactory` class that you can use directly, or you can specify your own `SSLFactory`.

Encryption

In addition to SSL (encryption on the transport layer), you can enable encryption of the content of the cluster events. You can use asymmetric encryption (with a public/private key-pair) or symmetric encryption (with a single key). You can configure this at a network element level in the `etc/hazelcast.xml` file.

The following example shows how to use symmetric encryption with a key generated for you by Hazelcast:

```
<hazelcast>
    ...
    <network>
        ...
        <!-- Make sure to set enabled=true
            Make sure this configuration is exactly the same on
            all members -->
        <symmetric-encryption enabled="true">
            <!--
                encryption algorithm such as
                DES/ECB/PKCS5Padding,
                PBEWithMD5AndDES,
                Blowfish,
                DESede
            -->
            <algorithm>PBEWithMD5AndDES</algorithm>
            <!-- salt value to use when generating the secret key
            -->
            <salt>thesalt</salt>
            <!-- pass phrase to use when generating the secret key
            -->
            <password>thepass</password>
            <!-- iteration count to use when generating the secret
            key -->
            <iteration-count>19</iteration-count>
        </symmetric-encryption>
    </network>
    ...
</hazelcast>
```

For asymmetric encryption, it's up to you to create the private/public key-pair using a keytool or openSSL.

The keys have to be stored in a keystore used in the `etc/hazelcast.xml` file:

```
<hazelcast>
    ...
    <network>
        ...
        <!--
            Make sure to set enabled=true
        -->
        <asymmetric-encryption enabled="true">
            <!-- encryption algorithm -->
            <algorithm>RSA/NONE/PKCS1PADDING</algorithm>
            <!-- private key password -->
            <keyPassword>thekeypass</keyPassword>
            <!-- private key alias -->
            <keyAlias>member1</keyAlias>
            <!-- key store type -->
            <storeType>JKS</storeType>
            <!-- key store password -->
            <storePassword>thestorepass</storePassword>
            <!-- path to the key store -->
            <storePath>keystore</storePath>
        </asymmetric-encryption>
    </network>
    ...
</hazelcast>
```

IPv6 support

You can directly use an IPv6 address format in the `etc/hazelcast.xml` file in the exact same location where you use the IPv4 format. This can be done with the following code:

```
<hazelcast>
    ...
    <network>
        <port auto-increment="true">5701</port>
        <join>
            <multicast enabled="false">
                <multicast-group>FF02:0:0:0:0:0:0:1
                </multicast-group>
                <multicast-port>54327</multicast-port>
            </multicast>
            <tcp-ip enabled="true">
```

```
        <member>[fe80::223:6cff:fe93:7c7e]:5701</member>
        <interface>192.168.1.0-7</interface>
        <interface>192.168.1.*</interface>
        <interface>fe80:0:0:0:45c5:47ee:fe15:493a
        </interface>
    </tcp-ip>
</join>
<interfaces enabled="true">
    <interface>10.3.16.*</interface>
    <interface>10.3.10.4-18</interface>
    <interface>fe80:0:0:0:45c5:47ee:fe15:*</interface>
    <interface>fe80::223:6cff:fe93:0-5555</interface>
</interfaces>
...
</network>
```

You can force the format of the IP addresses using the JVM's system property
(when your machine supports both):

- `java.net.preferIPv4Stack=<true|false>`
- `java.net.preferIPv6Addresses=<true|false>`

Restricting outbound ports

By default, the communication between nodes uses a random port number that
is created when the connection is established. Sometimes, it may be an issue
depending on the network security policy (firewalls, PAT, NAT, and so on). Instead
of random ports, you can define a ports' range or a list of ports to be used for the
communication between the nodes:

```
<hazelcast>
    ...
    <network>
        <port auto-increment="true">5701</port>
        <outbound-ports>
            <ports>33000-35000</ports>    <!-- ports between 33000
                and 35000 -->
            <ports>37000,37001,37002,37003</ports> <!-- comma
                separated ports -->
            <ports>38000,38500-38600</ports>
        </outbound-ports>
        ...
    </network>
    ...
</hazelcast>
```

The ports can be specified as a range (33000-35000 means that the ports in this range will be taken), as a list of ports separated by a comma and then delimited (38000, and so on), or as a mix of both.

Summary

In this chapter, we learned how Cellar and Hazelcast work together. We saw the usage of queue/topic for the communication between the nodes and the usage of map/set for the storage of the resources on the cluster. We saw how to tune the Cellar components in order to add persistence, limit the size of the elements, and perform other tasks.

We also learned how to extend the default Cellar Hazelcast configuration to match some additional requirements such as security.

The next chapter will introduce you to the cluster groups that allow you to group the nodes as per their names.

4
Cluster Groups

Until now, we have used Cellar as a global cluster. This means that all the nodes will have the same functions and roles in the cluster. However, when using a pool or farm of Karaf instances in a real live system, we may want to dedicate a subset of the instances for the given functions/roles. This is the role of the Cellar cluster groups.

For instance, we have a farm of 20 nodes in our Cellar cluster.

We may want to deploy the following:

- A camel route can be described and packaged as a `Karaf Features` XML file. We want to deploy this route only on 10 nodes of the cluster (not on all the nodes).
- A CXF web service (described and deployed as another `Karaf Features` XML file) on the other 10 nodes.

In Cellar, we can create different cluster groups and define a node as a member of one or more cluster groups.

Managing cluster groups

By default, all nodes are members of the default cluster group. This default cluster group is used as a template for the creation of new cluster groups.

You can create a cluster group using the `cluster:group-create <group-name>` command:

```
karaf@root> cluster:group-create book
```

Here, we created a new cluster group called `book`. We can see this new cluster group in the cluster groups' list with the `cluster:group-list` command:

```
karaf@root> cluster:group-list


   Group                   Members
* [default              ] [vostro.local:5701* ]
  [book                 ] []
```

For now, our `book` cluster group doesn't have any members.

A node can join a cluster group using the `cluster:group-join` command:

```
karaf@root>  cluster:group-join book
   Group                   Members
* [default              ] [vostro.local:5701* ]
* [book                 ] [vostro.local:5701* ]
```

The `cluster:group-join` command takes the following two arguments:

- The cluster group's name (in our example, the cluster group's name is `book`), as displayed by the `cluster:group-list` command.
- The node ID. In our example, we don't provide the node ID, meaning that the local node (the node that we are currently connected to) is used. It's also possible to provide a given node ID (for instance, a remote node) to join the cluster group using the following command:

  ```
  karaf@root> cluster:group-join book nodeB:5701
  ```

Thanks to this, you can control all the nodes and cluster groups from any node.

When a group is empty, you can delete it using the `cluster:group-delete <group_name>` command, as follows:

```
karaf@root> cluster:group-create test
karaf@root> cluster:group-list
   Group                   Members
  [default              ] []
  [test                 ] []
* [book                 ] [vostro.local:5701* ]
karaf@root> cluster:group-delete test
karaf@root> cluster:group-list
   Group                   Members
  [default              ] []
* [book                 ] [vostro.local:5701* ]
```

Note that the default cluster group cannot be deleted as it's used as a template to create new cluster groups. This means that the default configuration of the newly created cluster group will be a copy of the default cluster group configuration.

The `cluster:group-join` command adds a node to a given cluster group without changing the current cluster group's membership.

Thanks to this, a node can be a member of multiple cluster groups.

A node can quit a cluster group using the `cluster:group-quit` command:

```
karaf@root> cluster:group-list
    Group                Members
    [default           ] []
*   [test              ] [vostro.local:5701* ]
*   [book              ] [vostro.local:5701* ]
karaf@root> cluster:group-quit test
    Group                Members
    [default           ] []
    [test              ] []
*   [book              ] [vostro.local:5701* ]
```

The `cluster:group-set` command moves a node from one cluster group to another. It's a combination of the `cluster:group-join` and `cluster:group-quit` commands:

```
karaf@root> cluster:group-list
    Group                Members
    [default           ] []
    [test              ] []
*   [book              ] [vostro.local:5701* ]
karaf@root> cluster:group-set test
    Group                Members
    [default           ] []
*   [test              ] [vostro.local:5701* ]
    [book              ] []
```

Targeting provisioning

Once you have created your cluster groups and assigned nodes to the different cluster groups, you can target the deployment of the resources on a given cluster group. For this, Cellar provides the cluster-aware commands of the regular Karaf commands.

For instance, Karaf provides a `features:install <feature_name>` command to install a Karaf feature in the container. Additionally, Cellar provides `cluster:feature-install <group_name> <feature_name>`, which is similar to the `features:install` command. The `features:install` command will install the feature locally to the Karaf container, whereas the `cluster:feature-install` command will install the feature on the cluster in the given cluster group.

At the end of this chapter, you will find a table that introduces Cellar's `cluster:*` commands which correspond to the regular Karaf commands.

Features

In order to deploy a feature to a given cluster group, we can use the `cluster:feature-install` command:

```
karaf@root> cluster:feature-install book eventadmin
```

The `cluster:feature-install` command accepts the following arguments:

- The cluster group's name (here, `book`)
- The feature's name (here, `eventadmin`)
- The feature's version (optional)

For instance, we installed the `eventadmin` feature on the `book` cluster group. As Cellar extends the regular Karaf commands, we will find the exact same functions prefixed to the cluster.

You can control the Karaf feature repositories (URLs) per cluster group. For instance, you can list the Karaf feature repositories that are registered and available on a cluster group with the following command:

```
karaf@root> cluster:feature-url-list book
mvn:org.apache.karaf.cellar/apache-karaf-cellar/2.3.1/xml/features
mvn:org.jclouds.karaf/jclouds-karaf/1.4.0/xml/features
mvn:org.apache.karaf.assemblies.features/standard/2.3.1/xml/features
mvn:org.apache.karaf.assemblies.features/enterprise/2.3.1/xml/features
```

You can add a feature's URL on a cluster group using `cluster:feature-url-add`.

For instance, you can add the Camel feature repository on the `book` cluster group with the following commands:

```
karaf@root> cluster:feature-url-add book mvn:org.apache.camel.karaf/
apache-camel/2.12.1/xml/features
karaf@root> cluster:feature-url-list book
```

```
mvn:org.apache.karaf.cellar/apache-karaf-cellar/2.3.1/xml/features
mvn:org.jclouds.karaf/jclouds-karaf/1.4.0/xml/features
mvn:org.apache.karaf.assemblies.features/standard/2.3.1/xml/features
mvn:org.apache.karaf.assemblies.features/enterprise/2.3.1/xml/features
mvn:org.apache.camel.karaf/apache-camel/2.12.1/xml/features
```

This means that all the node members of the book cluster group will register the features repository locally. Using the regular Karaf commands (local), we can see the features repository, as follows:

```
karaf@root> features:listurl
  Loaded    URI
    true    mvn:org.apache.karaf.cellar/apache-karaf-cellar/2.3.1/xml/
features
    true    mvn:org.jclouds.karaf/jclouds-karaf/1.4.0/xml/features
    true    mvn:org.apache.karaf.assemblies.features/standard/2.3.1/xml/
features
    true    mvn:org.apache.karaf.assemblies.features/enterprise/2.3.1/xml/
features
    true    mvn:org.apache.camel.karaf/apache-camel/2.12.1/xml/features
```

Now, we can see that the Camel features are available on both the book cluster group (which we can list with the cluster:feature-list command) and locally on a node member of the book cluster group (which we can list with features:listurl). This can be done by issuing the following command:

```
karaf@root> cluster:feature-list book
...
[uninstalled] [2.12.1         ] camel-cxf
[uninstalled] [3.0.7.RELEASE  ] spring-orm
[uninstalled] [2.12.1         ] camel-apns
[uninstalled] [2.12.1         ] camel-guice
```

Bundles

Cellar also provides cluster-aware bundle commands. You can see the bundles that are available on a cluster group using the cluster:bundle-list command (equivalent to the osgi:list Karaf command), as follows:

```
karaf@root> cluster:bundle-list book
...

[59  ] [Active    ] Apache Karaf :: Features :: Management (2.3.1)
[60  ] [Active    ] Apache Karaf :: Features :: Core (2.3.1)
```

```
[61  ] [Active   ] Apache Karaf :: Cellar :: Bundle (2.3.1)
[62  ] [Active   ] Apache Karaf :: Shell :: PackageAdmin Commands (2.3.1)
[63  ] [Active   ] Apache Karaf :: Deployer :: Karaf Archive (.kar)
(2.3.1)
```

We can deploy a bundle on a cluster group using the `cluster:bundle-install` command (equivalent to the `osgi:install` Karaf command):

```
karaf@root> cluster:bundle-install book mvn:org.apache.servicemix.
bundles/org.apache.servicemix.bundles.commons-lang/2.4_6

karaf@root> cluster:bundle-list book|grep -i commons-lang

[64  ] [Installed ] Apache ServiceMix :: Bundles :: commons-lang
(2.4.0.6)
```

The applications of the cluster-aware bundle commands are listed as follows:

- To see the bundle that is installed locally on a node member of the book cluster group, you can use the following command:

  ```
  karaf@root> osgi:list|grep -i commons-lang

  [  64] [Installed ] [           ] [   80] Apache ServiceMix ::
  Bundles :: commons-lang (2.4.0.6)
  ```

- To start a bundle on the cluster, you can use the `cluster:bundle-start` command. If you want to start the bundle with the ID 64 on the cluster (found using the `cluster:bundle-list` command), issue the following commands:

  ```
  karaf@root> cluster:bundle-start book 64

  karaf@root> cluster:bundle-list book|grep -i commons-lang

  [64  ] [Active   ] Apache ServiceMix :: Bundles :: commons-lang
  (2.4.0.6)
  ```

- To stop a bundle on a given cluster group, you can use the `cluster:bundle-stop` command. You can use the `osgi:list` command to see the local status of the bundles:

  ```
  karaf@root> cluster:bundle-stop book 64

  karaf@root> osgi:list|grep -i commons-lang

  [  64] [Installed ] [           ] [   80] Apache ServiceMix ::
  Bundles :: commons-lang (2.4.0.6)
  ```

- To uninstall a bundle from a cluster group, you can use the `cluster:bundle-uninstall` command:

  ```
  karaf@root> cluster:bundle-uninstall book 64
  ```

Configurations

Cellar allows clustering of configurations. You can use the `cluster:config-*` commands to manage the configurations on the cluster.

You can list the configurations available on a given cluster group using the `cluster:config-list` command:

```
karaf@root> cluster:config-list book

...

-------------------------------------------------------------

Pid:          org.apache.karaf.features.obr
Properties:
   startLevel = 80
   startByDefault = true
   service.pid = org.apache.karaf.features.obr
   resolveOptionalImports = false
```

You can edit or change a property (using the `cluster:config-propset` command), add a property (using the `cluster:config-propappend` command), delete a property (using the `cluster:config-propdel` command), or list the properties of a configuration on a given cluster group, as follows:

```
karaf@root> cluster:config-propappend book my.config key value
karaf@root> cluster:config-proplist book my.config
Property list for configuration PID my.config in cluster group book
Key                             Value
key                             value
service.pid                     my.config
karaf@root> cluster:config-propdel book my.config key
karaf@root> cluster:config-proplist book my.config
Property list for configuration PID my.config in cluster group book
Key                             Value
service.pid                     my.config
```

Optional resources

Features, bundles, and configurations are natively supported by Cellar. However, by installing optional features, Cellar can provide clustering support for other resources too.

The **OSGi Bundle Repository (OBR)** is an OSGi specification with the following goals:

- To simplify the deployment of bundles
- To encourage independent and atomic bundle development

OBR uses a bundle repository where it can add some additional metadata as follows:

- The capabilities provided by a bundle
- The requirements of a bundle

Thanks to this metadata, when you install a bundle from an OBR server, OBR automatically installs the other bundles providing the capabilities to match the requirements of the first bundle that you have installed.

The `cellar-obr` feature provides support for cluster-aware OBR. This means that Cellar synchronizes the OBR servers used between the different nodes and broadcasts the OBR commands (install, start, uninstall, and so on) between the nodes in the cluster.

We can find the `cluster:obr-*` commands dedicated to the clustered OBR.

The `cellar-eventadmin` feature doesn't provide new commands. However, all OSGi local events are broadcasted on the cluster to the other node members of the same cluster group as the local node.

Overlapping

A node can be a member of several cluster groups. This means that we may have an overlap (on a single node) between multiple cluster groups, which can be seen in the following diagram:

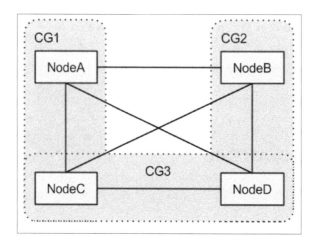

If we install a feature on the cluster group **CG1** (with the `cluster:feature-install cg1 feature` command), the feature will be installed locally on **NodeA** and **NodeC**. As **NodeC** is a member of the cluster group **CG3**, the feature will be installed on **NodeD** (a member of the cluster group **CG3**) by transitivity. Again, as **NodeD** is a member of the cluster group **CG2** and as **NodeB** is also a member of this cluster group, the feature will be installed on **NodeB** too. This means that the feature will be installed on all the cluster groups, and thereby on all the nodes.

Generally speaking, a best practice is to avoid the possession of a node member of several cluster groups, or you may encounter its side effect—the feature will be installed on all the nodes (irrespective of what their cluster group is), whereas the user may expect the feature to be installed only on the cluster group **CG1**.

The summary of commands

The following table summarizes the local commands (natively provided by Karaf) and the corresponding commands dedicated for the cluster (provided by Cellar):

Local commands	Cluster commands
`features:listurl`	`cluster:feature-url-list`
`features:addurl`	`cluster:feature-url-add`
`features:removeurl`	`cluster:feature-url-remove`
`features:list`	`cluster:feature-list`
`features:install`	`cluster:feature-install`
`features:uninstall`	`cluster:feature-uninstall`
`osgi:list`	`cluster:bundle-list`
`osgi:install`	`cluster:bundle-install`
`osgi:uninstall`	`cluster:bundle-uninstall`
`osgi:start`	`cluster:bundle-start`
`osgi:stop`	`cluster:bundle-stop`
`config:list`	`cluster:config-list`
`config:delete`	`cluster:config-delete`
`config:propset`	`cluster:config-propset`
`config:propappend`	`cluster:config-propappend`
`config:propdel`	`cluster:config-propdel`
`config:proplist`	`cluster:config-proplist`
`obr:addurl`	`cluster:obr-add-url`
`obr:deploy`	`cluster:obr-deploy`
`obr:list`	`cluster:obr-list`
`obr:listurl`	`cluster:obr-list-url`
`obr:removeurl`	`cluster:obr-remove-url`

All actions performed by the `cluster:*` commands can be performed via JMX using MBeans, provided by Cellar. On the other hand, it's also possible to manage a cluster group using a WebConsole plugin provided by Cellar.

Summary

In this chapter, we saw how to group nodes and target the provisioning on a specific cluster group. Thanks to this, it's easy to set up a multilayered cluster and to group the nodes per function.

In the next chapter, we will see the different Cellar components that are used to create and transport the cluster events between the members of the same cluster groups; we will also see how a group is actually implemented.

5
Producers, Consumers, Handlers, Listeners, and Synchronizers

In the previous chapters, we saw that Cellar exchanges cluster events between different nodes. This means that a node creates a cluster event and sends it to the other nodes. On the other hand, the other nodes receive the cluster events and update the local state with the statements contained in the cluster events.

Beneath the hood, a node acts as a cluster event producer. Cellar uses a Hazelcast queue to store and dispatch the cluster event to the other nodes. A producer sends a message that represents a cluster event to the queue.

The other nodes act as cluster event consumers. This means that they consume the cluster event from the queue. As the queue contains different cluster event types (a bundle event, a configuration event, a feature event, and an OBR event), the consumer delegates the handling of the event to a handler dedicated for each kind of cluster event. This process is shown in the following diagram:

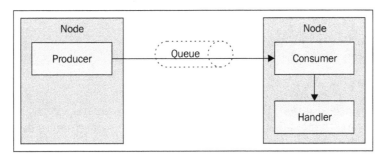

The event producer

Each Cellar node embeds a cluster event producer. The producer is used when the node has to send an event to the other nodes.

The producer is responsible for the following functions:

- To create the cluster event message.
- To send the cluster event message in a target distributed queue. The queue is unique and can be identified by the cluster group and the type of resource. For instance, a possible queue name is `book.bundles`, where `book` is the cluster group's name and `bundles` is the type of the resource. Thanks to this, Cellar is able to send a cluster event per resource and is able to target this cluster event only to a given cluster group.

It's possible to manage the producer of a node from any node.

For instance, we can see the current status of the producer using the following `cluster:producer-status` command:

```
karaf@root> cluster:producer-status
   Node                         Status
   [node2:5702          ] [ON   ]
 * [node1:5701          ] [ON   ]
```

Here, we can see the status of the producer of all the nodes in the global cluster. We can specify a node with the following command:

```
karaf@root> cluster:producer-status node2:5702
   Node                         Status
   [node2:5702          ] [ON   ]
```

It's possible to stop the producer of a node using the `cluster:producer-stop` command (without argument, this command stops the producer of the local node), as follows:

```
karaf@root> cluster:producer-stop node2:5702
   Node                         Status
   [node2:5702          ] [OFF  ]
```

When a producer is stopped, the node doesn't send any cluster events to the other nodes. This means that local changes and the `cluster:*` commands don't change the other nodes in the cluster.

The cluster:producer-stop command can stop a producer located on a remote node (distant from the node on which we actually execute the command).

You can start the stopped producer using the cluster:producer-start command, as follows:

```
karaf@root> cluster:producer-start node2:5702
    Node                        Status
    [node2:5702          ] [ON   ]
```

A producer can send any kind of cluster events. Each clustered resource has its own kind of cluster event. The following are the types of cluster events:

- ClusterBundleEvent: This is sent when the state of a bundle changes (install, start, stop, or uninstall)

- ClusterFeatureEvent: This is sent when the state of a Karaf feature changes (add repository, remove repository, install, or uninstall)

- ClusterConfigEvent: This is sent when the state of a configuration changes (delete, add, set property, delete property, or append property)

- ClusterObrEvent: This is sent when the state of an OBR bundle changes (add repository, deploy OBR bundle, or start OBR bundle)

The cluster:producer-start and cluster:producer-stop commands update the etc/org.apache.karaf.cellar.node.cfg configuration file.

This configuration file contains the producer property that defines the state of the producer (used at startup for instance): if the producer's state is true, the node producer is started, else the producer is stopped.

The event consumer

As explained before, a producer sends a cluster event message in a queue.

On the other hand, each node embeds a consumer. A consumer binds a set of handlers.

The consumer is responsible to get the cluster event messages from the different queues, and depending on the type of the cluster event, the consumer delegates the cluster event to a handler. This means that you have a handler for every type of resource.

For a consumer, we can perform the following tasks:

- Check the current status of the consumer (on each node) using the `cluster:consumer-status` command, as follows:

```
karaf@root> cluster:consumer-status
    Node                           Status
    [node2:5702            ] [ON  ]
  * [node1:5701            ] [ON  ]
```

  The `cluster:consumer-status` command accepts a node ID as the argument, as follows:

```
karaf@root>  cluster:consumer-status node2:5702
    Node                           Status
    [node2:5702            ] [ON  ]
```

- Stop the consumer of any node using the `cluster:consumer-stop` command, as follows:

```
karaf@root> cluster:consumer-stop node2:5702
    Node                           Status
    [node2:5702            ] [OFF ]
```

  When a consumer is stopped on a node, the node can't receive any cluster events coming from another node. This means that the node won't update its local state with the information contained in the cluster event's message.

- Start the consumer of any node using the `cluster:consumer-start` command, as follows:

```
karaf@root> cluster:consumer-start node2:5702
    Node                           Status
    [node2:5702            ] [ON  ]
```

Similar to the status of the producer, the status of the consumer is stored in the `consumer` property of the `etc/org.apache.karaf.cellar.node.cfg` configuration file.

Event handlers

When the consumer receives a cluster event's message, it delegates the message to a handler depending on the type of the cluster event.

You have one handler per type of resource that Cellar manages. The following is a list of the event handlers:

- `ConfigurationEventHandler`: This is responsible for handling cluster events related to configurations (for instance, events that come from the `cluster:config-*` or `config:*` commands)

- `BundleEventHandler`: This is responsible for handling cluster events related to bundles (for instance, events that come from the `cluster:bundle-*` or `osgi:*` commands)

- `FeaturesEventHandler`: This is responsible for handling cluster events related to features (for instance, events that come from the `cluster:feature-*` or `features:*` commands)

- `ObrBundleEventHandler` and `ObrUrlEventHandler` (optional): These are responsible for handling cluster events related to the OBR service (for instance, events that come from the `cluster:obr-*` or `obr:*` commands)

- `ClusterEventHandler` (optional): This is responsible for handling cluster events related to the `eventadmin` service

You can see the list of the handlers and their current statuses using the `cluster:handler-status` command, as follows:

```
karaf@root> cluster:handler-status

   Node                          Status   Event Handler
   [node2:5702            ]  [ON   ]  org.apache.karaf.cellar.config.
ConfigurationEventHandler
   [node2:5702            ]  [ON   ]  org.apache.karaf.cellar.bundle.
BundleEventHandler
   [node2:5702            ]  [ON   ]  org.apache.karaf.cellar.features.
FeaturesEventHandler
 * [node1:5701            ]  [ON   ]  org.apache.karaf.cellar.config.
ConfigurationEventHandler
 * [node1:5701            ]  [ON   ]  org.apache.karaf.cellar.bundle.
BundleEventHandler
 * [node1:5701            ]  [ON   ]  org.apache.karaf.cellar.features.
FeaturesEventHandler
```

You can stop a specific handler on any node using the `cluster:handler-stop` command. The `cluster:handler-stop` command takes the following two arguments:

- The event handler's class name
- The node ID to stop the event handler (optional)

The result of using the `cluster:handler-stop` command is as follows:

```
karaf@root> cluster:handler-stop org.apache.karaf.cellar.bundle.
BundleEventHandler node2:5702
      Node                      Status  Event Handler
    [node2:5702              ] [OFF  ] org.apache.karaf.cellar.bundle.
BundleEventHandler
```

When a handler is stopped on a node, it means that the cluster events that are managed by the handler are not processed. For instance, if `BundleEventHandler` is stopped, the node will receive cluster events, but the cluster events that are related to the bundle will not be processed. This means that the node won't change the bundle's status.

You can start a handler on any node using the `cluster:handler-start` command as follows:

```
karaf@root> cluster:handler-start org.apache.karaf.cellar.bundle.
BundleEventHandler node2:5702
      Node                      Status  Event Handler
    [node2:5702              ] [ON   ] org.apache.karaf.cellar.bundle.
BundleEventHandler
```

Similar to the statuses of a producer and a consumer, the status of each handler is stored in the `etc/org.apache.karaf.cellar.node.cfg` configuration file, as follows:

```
#
# Cluster event handlers
#
# bundle event handler
handler.org.apache.karaf.cellar.bundle.BundleEventHandler = true
# config event handler
handler.org.apache.karaf.cellar.config.ConfigurationEventHandler = true
# feature event handler
handler.org.apache.karaf.cellar.features.FeaturesEventHandler = true
# DOSGi event handler
handler.org.apache.karaf.cellar.dosgi.RemoteServiceCallHandler = true
# OSGi event handler
handler.org.apache.karaf.cellar.event.ClusterEventHandler = true
# OBR event handler
handler.org.apache.karaf.cellar.obr.ObrBundleEventHandler = true
handler.org.apache.karaf.cellar.obr.ObrUrlEventHandler = true
```

Listeners and synchronizers

If we use the `cluster:*` commands to manage the resources in the cluster (features, bundles, configurations, OBR, and local events), Cellar also listens to the changes in the local resources and broadcasts these changes in the cluster.

For instance, if you install a bundle locally (using the `osgi:install` command), Cellar will catch this change and broadcast it in the cluster event, meaning that all other nodes in the same cluster group as the local node will install the same bundle.

Cellar provides the following listeners:

- A listener for the features repository and features (install and uninstall)
- A listener for bundles (install, uninstall, start, stop, and so on)
- A listener for configurations (propset, propdel, delete, and so on)

On the other hand, when a node starts or joins a cluster group, Cellar invokes a set of synchronizers. The purpose of a synchronizer is to align the local state of the node with the state of the resources in the cluster. A synchronizer is responsible for applying local changes to have the node in the same state as in the cluster. You have one synchronizer per resource type.

Cellar provides the following synchronizers:

- A synchronizer for the features repository and features. For instance, if a feature has the status `installed` on the cluster, the synchronizer (at startup) checks the state of the feature on the local node, and if the feature is not installed, the synchronizer installs it.
- A synchronizer for bundles. For instance, if a bundle is installed on the cluster, the synchronizer (at startup) checks the state of the bundle on the local node, and if the bundle is not installed, the synchronizer installs it.
- A synchronizer for configurations.

Thanks to these synchronizers, Cellar updates a node when it starts or joins a cluster group.

Summary

Cellar provides complete control over the different components involved in the communication between the nodes. Thanks to this, a user can define the behavior of each node by starting or stopping the event consumers, producers, and handlers.

Additional to node behavior, we can also filter the cluster events exchanged in the cluster, as we will see in the next chapter.

6
The Filtering of Cluster Events

In the previous chapter, we saw how cluster events are created and transported using producers, consumers, and handlers. We saw that we have one internal queue managed per resource (bundle, feature, and configuration) and per cluster group. This allows us to group the nodes and target the provisioning of a resource on a specific group. So, it's the first kind of filtering at the node level.

In this chapter, we will cover the following topics:

- How to filter the cluster events in a given cluster group
- How to define the resources (bundles, features, configurations, and OBRs) to be filtered
- How to define the direction of the filter (coming in or going out from the nodes)

The configuration of the filters

The filtering of cluster events is defined in the `etc/org.apache.karaf.cellar.groups.cfg` configuration file. In this configuration file, you can find the filters with the following format:

```
cluster_group.[bundle|config|features].[whitelist|blacklist].
[inbound|outbound]=regex
```

For instance, the following configuration blocks (`blacklist`) the incoming cluster events (`inbound`) that contain features named `my-feature` or `other-*` in the `default` cluster group:

```
default.features.blacklist.inbound=my-feature,other-*
```

Cellar provides a default filtering configuration for the `default` cluster group. This configuration is used as a template when you create a new cluster group. You can update the filters' configuration live by directly modifying the configuration on the node or using the `config:*` and `cluster:config-*` commands.

For instance, to add a new filter to a cluster group, you can run the following commands:

```
karaf@root> config:edit org.apache.karaf.cellar.groups
karaf@root> config:propset mygroup.bundle.blacklist.outbound none
karaf@root> config:update
```

You can also use ConfigMBean to update the configuration remotely (using JConsole for instance).

The name of the cluster group is `cluster_group`, which you provided in the `cluster:group-create` command.

Resources

In the previous chapter, we saw that we have an internal queue per resource and per cluster group.

A resource is a type of a cluster event. Cellar defines the following cluster events:

- `bundle`: This is a cluster event that corresponds to a bundle action (install, uninstall, start, stop, and so on)
- `config`: This is a cluster event that corresponds to a configuration action (create, delete, propset, propappend, propdel, and so on)
- `features`: This is a cluster event that corresponds to a feature action (addurl, delurl, install, uninstall, and so on)

Remember that each type of cluster event is managed by a specific handler.

In the filter definition, specify the resource just after `cluster_group`. This will allow you to filter the events of a specific type (`bundle`, `config`, and `features`).

Blacklist and whitelist

In the filter definition, you can specify the `blacklist` or `whitelist` keyword after the resource. A blacklisted filter will block the corresponding cluster events. This means that the cluster events won't be delivered on the cluster. On the other hand, a whitelisted filter will allow the corresponding cluster events. The filter is built by evaluating the whitelist first and by overriding the blacklist later. With the combination of blacklist and whitelist filters, you can define fine-grained filtering.

Inbound and outbound

Another property used to configure filters is the direction of the cluster event. The two directions can be distinguished as follows:

- `inbound`: The `inbound` cluster events are the events that come into a node. These cluster events come from another node and enter other nodes.

- `outbound`: The `outbound` cluster events are the events that go out of a node. These cluster events are produced and sent from a node to other nodes.

Thanks to inbound and outbound filters, you can filter the same cluster event depending on its direction: incoming or outgoing.

Regex and event identification

Finally, we have to specify the cluster event. The purpose is to allow (`whitelist`) or block (`blacklist`) specific cluster events. For instance, we want to block the following:

- The cluster event that contains a change in the feature named `my-feature`
- The cluster event that contains a change in the bundle named `my-bundle`

So, we have to identify and declare the cluster event. To identify a cluster event, we can use the following:

- The event identifier can be used; for instance, `org.apache.karaf.cellar.groups` identifies the configuration's cluster event (PID).

- A **regular expression** (**regex**) or glob based on the event identifier can be used. Declaring events using the full qualified name can be tedious. The usage of a regex is much faster. For instance, `org.apache.karaf.cellar.*` identified all the configuration cluster events containing PIDs.

- `*` selects all cluster events.

- The `none` keyword is a reserved keyword to not select any cluster event.

The identification depends on the resource of the cluster event filter.

Bundle

For a bundle cluster event, the identifier is the bundle's location. You can get the bundle's location using the `osgi:list -l` command, which will give you the following output:

```
...
[  61] [Active      ] [Created ] [   40]
mvn:org.apache.karaf.cellar/org.apache.karaf.cellar.features/2.3.2
[  62] [Active      ] [Created ] [   40]
mvn:org.apache.karaf.cellar/org.apache.karaf.cellar.management/2.3.2
[  70] [Active      ] [           ] [   30]
mvn:org.apache.felix/org.apache.felix.eventadmin/1.3.2
```

For instance, if you want to block (filter) all the bundle cluster events, both `inbound` and `outbound`, for the `eventadmin` bundle in the `my` cluster group, you can specify the following filter in the `etc/org.apache.karaf.cellar.groups.cfg` configuration file:

```
my.bundle.blacklist.inbound=mvn:org.apache.felix/org.apache.felix.
eventadmin/1.3.2
```

```
my.bundle.blacklist.outbound=mvn:org.apache.felix/org.apache.felix.
eventadmin/1.3.2
```

This is where regex is very useful. We can simplify the filter as follows:

```
my.bundle.blacklist.inbound=*org.apache.felix.eventadmin*
```

```
my.bundle.blacklist.outbound=*org.apache.felix.eventadmin*
```

Configuration

For the configuration cluster event, the identifier is the configuration PID. You can get the configuration PID using the `config:list` command.

By default, Cellar blacklists its own configuration and avoids syncing the configurations that are only valid locally to a node. The following is how this configuration will look in the `etc/org.apache.karaf.cellar.groups.cfg` configuration file:

```
default.config.whitelist.inbound = *
default.config.whitelist.outbound = *
default.config.blacklist.inbound = org.apache.felix.fileinstall*,
\
                                    org.apache.karaf.cellar*, \
                                    org.apache.karaf.management, \
                                    org.apache.karaf.shell, \
                                    org.ops4j.pax.logging, \
                                    org.ops4j.pax.web
default.config.blacklist.outbound = org.apache.felix.fileinstall*,
\
                                    org.apache.karaf.cellar*, \
                                    org.apache.karaf.management, \
                                    org.apache.karaf.shell, \
                                    org.ops4j.pax.logging, \
                                    org.ops4j.pax.web
```

The following is an explanation of the configurations in the preceding code snippet:

- The `org.apache.felix.fileinstall*` configurations are excluded (inbound and outbound) as the polled directories are local to the node (so, it doesn't make sense to spread this configuration to the `default` cluster group)

- The `org.apache.karaf.cellar*` configurations are excluded as they are provided by Cellar itself

- The `org.apache.karaf.management` configuration is excluded as it contains the port number of the Karaf JMX MBean server (so it is local to a node)

- The `org.apache.karaf.shell` configuration is excluded as it contains the port number of the Karaf SSHd server (so it is local to a node)

- The `org.ops4j.pax.logging` configuration is excluded to be able to change the log level of a node without changing the log levels on the other nodes

- The `org.ops4j.pax.web` configuration is excluded as it contains the port number of the Karaf HTTP service (so it is local to a node)

Features

For the features cluster event, the identifier is the name of the feature. You can get the feature names using the `features:list` command, which will give you the following output:

```
...
[uninstalled] [2.3.2            ] cellar-webconsole
     karaf-cellar-2.3.2  Cellar plugin for Karaf WebConsole
[uninstalled] [1.0.1            ] transaction
     karaf-enterprise-2.3.1 OSGi Transaction Manager
[uninstalled] [1.0.1            ] jpa
     karaf-enterprise-2.3.1 OSGi Persistence Container
[uninstalled] [1.0.0            ] jndi
     karaf-enterprise-2.3.1 OSGi Service Registry JNDI access
[uninstalled] [1.0.0            ] application-without-isolation
     karaf-enterprise-2.3.1 Provide EBA archive support
```

By default, Cellar blacklists some features as follows:

```
default.features.whitelist.inbound = *
default.features.whitelist.outbound = *
default.features.blacklist.inbound =
config,management,hazelcast,cellar*
default.features.blacklist.outbound =
config,management,hazelcast,cellar*
```

The Hazelcast and Cellar features are installed by Cellar itself; so, there is no need to handle the cluster events for these features. That's why the `default` filter configuration allows all the cluster feature events except the `config`, `management`, `hazelcast`, and all the Cellar (`cellar*`) features.

On the other hand, the `config` and `management` features are provided by default by Karaf. As these are very low-level features, these are not required to handle the events for these features.

The default filter configuration

Cellar uses the following default filter configuration:

```
default.config.whitelist.inbound = *
default.config.whitelist.outbound = *
default.config.blacklist.inbound = org.apache.felix.fileinstall*,
\
                                    org.apache.karaf.cellar*, \
                                    org.apache.karaf.management, \
                                    org.apache.karaf.shell, \
                                    org.ops4j.pax.logging, \
                                    org.ops4j.pax.web
default.config.blacklist.outbound = org.apache.felix.fileinstall*,
\
                                     org.apache.karaf.cellar*, \
                                     org.apache.karaf.management, \
                                     org.apache.karaf.shell, \
                                     org.ops4j.pax.logging, \
                                     org.ops4j.pax.web

default.features.whitelist.inbound = *
default.features.whitelist.outbound = *
default.features.blacklist.inbound =
config,management,hazelcast,cellar*
default.features.blacklist.outbound =
config,management,hazelcast,cellar*

default.bundle.whitelist.inbound = *
default.bundle.whitelist.outbound = *
default.bundle.blacklist.inbound = none
default.bundle.blacklist.outbound = none
```

The following is the explanation of the preceding configuration:

- All the cluster `configuration` events are allowed (`whitelist`) in the `default` cluster group (`inbound` and `outbound`) for the node, except (`blacklist`) the configurations with the `org.apache.felix.fileinstall*`, `org.apache.karaf.cellar*`, `org.apache.karaf.management`, `org.apache.karaf.shell`, `org.ops4j.pax.logging`, and `org.ops4j.pax.web` PIDs.

- All the cluster `feature` events are allowed (`whitelist`) in the `default` cluster group, `inbound` and `outbound` to the node, except (`blacklist`) the features named `config`, `management`, `hazelcast`, and `cellar*`.

- All the cluster `bundle` events are allowed (`whitelist`) in the `default` cluster group, which are `inbound` and `outbound` to the node. No bundles are blocked (`blacklist` is `none`).

Summary

In this chapter, we learned how to configure the filtering of cluster events. It provides fine-grained management of the cluster events: per cluster group, per direction (inbound or outbound), per resource (feature, bundle, and config), supporting regex to identify the cluster events, and type of filtering (whitelist or blacklist).

It also allows the cluster administrator to define which resources should be synchronized on the cluster.

In the next chapter, we will see another application for resource synchronization: remote communication between bundles using **Distributed OSGi (DOSGi)**.

DOSGi

In the previous chapters, we saw Cellar as a provisioning clustering solution; the actions performed on resources from one node create cluster events that are sent to the other nodes; these nodes then react accordingly. Cellar also provides some features in addition to the provisioning cluster. Cellar **Distributed OSGi (DOSGi)** is one of these additional features.

In this chapter, we will cover the following topics:

- What DOSGi is and a use case
- The Cellar DOSGi implementation
- A complete example using Cellar DOSGi

What is Cellar DOSGi?

Cellar DOSGi is an implementation of the Remote Service Admin specifications from the OSGi specifications. Basically, it's a remote communication between services from bundles hosted in different containers.

With the OSGi service, a bundle exposes a service (actually, an interface) to the service registry provided by the OSGi framework. Another bundle can look up for services in the service registry, get a reference to this service, and use it. Thanks to this, we have a real **Service-Oriented Architecture (SOA)** approach on low-level components (bundles).

Cellar DOSGi brings a distributed service registry and remote usage of a service using Hazelcast NIO.

Hazelcast NIO is a data serialization and transport implementation of NIO. For details, you can take a look at the Java NIO Javadocs (`http://docs.oracle.com/javase/7/docs/api/java/nio/package-summary.html`) and Hazelcast NIO documentation (`http://hazelcast.org/docs/2.6/javadoc/com/hazelcast/nio/DataSerializable.html`).

The following diagram shows how two nodes communicate with each other via a distributed service registry:

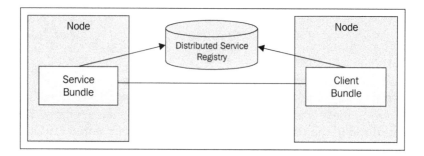

On a node, a bundle (named the **Service Bundle**) can expose a service in the distributed service registry. To do this, it just registers the service with the `service.exported.interfaces` service property. We will see how to create a service and define this service property using an example later in this chapter. Cellar listens for all service registrations, and if a service has the `service.exported.interfaces` property, it automatically exposes it to the distributed service registry.

On the other hand, a bundle (named the **Client Bundle**) just does a regular service lookup. Cellar intercepts this lookup under the following circumstances:

- If the service exists in the local service registry, Cellar uses it
- If the service doesn't exist in the local service registry, Cellar forwards the lookup to the distributed service registry

The client bundle gets a reference to the service. In the case of a local service, this reference is directly to the object in the JVM. In the case of a remote service, this reference is a proxy to the actual service located in a remote JVM.

We have to note that DOSGi doesn't use cluster groups (cluster groups are used in resources synchronization for now). This means that node members of different cluster groups can communicate with each other using DOSGi.

To illustrate and understand (from a user's standpoint) how Cellar DOSGi works, we will create a Greeter application.

In this application, we will have a bundle that exposes a service by saying `hello` and a client bundle that uses this service.

The source code of the example is available in Cellar sources at the following link:

```
https://github.com/apache/karaf-cellar/tree/cellar-2.3.x/samples/
dosgi-greeter
```

The API bundle

In OSGi, a service is described with an interface. This means that both service and client bundles of the same service have to share the same interface.

In order to decouple interface and implementation and be able to update a client bundle without impacting a service bundle, a good practice is to create an API bundle that contains just the interface.

We create this API bundle by just exposing the API package in the OSGi export package header as follows:

```
<osgi.export>
  org.apache.karaf.cellar.samples.dosgi.greeter.
api*;version="${project.version}"
</osgi.export>
```

The API bundle contains the interface that describes the Greeter service as follows:

```
package org.apache.karaf.cellar.samples.dosgi.greeter.api;

/**
 * Interface describing the Greeter service.
 */
public interface Greeter {

  /**
   * Returns a greet message.
   * @return
   */
  public GreetResponse greet(Greet greet);

}
```

The service provides an operation: `greet` corresponding to the `greet()` method of the Greeter interface. This `greet()` method takes an object as an argument (`Greet`) and returns an object (`GreetResponse`).

These objects are also part of the API bundle, as they will be used by both service and client bundles. The `Greet` object just wraps a message (a string). Note that this object is serializable. This is required as it will be used remotely. The message can be wrapped with the following code:

```
package org.apache.karaf.cellar.samples.dosgi.greeter.api;

import java.io.Serializable;

/**
 * Object used in the Greeter interface/service.
 */
public class Greet implements Serializable {
  String message;

  public Greet(String message) {
      this.message = message;
  }

  public String getMessage() {
      return message;
  }

  public void setMessage(String message) {
      this.message = message;
  }

}
```

The `GreetResponse` class represents the response returned by the `greet()` method. It's also a `Serializable` object, as it will be transported between the nodes (remotely). This is done with the following code:

```
package org.apache.karaf.cellar.samples.dosgi.greeter.api;

import java.io.Serializable;

/**
 * Response returned by the Greeter service.
 */
public class GreetResponse implements Serializable {

  private Greet greet;
  private String response;
```

```
public GreetResponse(Greet greet, String response) {
    this.greet = greet;
    this.response = response;
}

public Greet getGreet() {
    return greet;
}

public void setGreet(Greet greet) {
    this.greet = greet;
}

public String getResponse() {
    return response;
}

public void setResponse(String response) {
    this.response = response;
}

}
```

The API bundle doesn't provide the implementation of the Greet service. It's just the API.

The implementation and the registration of the service are done in the service bundle.

The service bundle

The service bundle exposes a service to the service registry.

A service will be exposed to the distributed service registry just by adding the service.exported.interfaces property to the service.

First, the service bundle implements the Greet interface; it's the implementation of the Greet service, which is as follows:

```
package org.apache.karaf.cellar.samples.dosgi.greeter.service;

import org.apache.karaf.cellar.samples.dosgi.greeter.api.Greet;
import
  org.apache.karaf.cellar.samples.dosgi.greeter.api.GreetResponse;
import org.apache.karaf.cellar.samples.dosgi.greeter.api.Greeter;
```

```
/**
 * Implementation of the Greeter service.
 */
public class GreeterImpl implements Greeter {

    private int counter=0;
    private String id;

    public GreeterImpl(String id) {
        this.id = id;
    }

    @Override
    public GreetResponse greet(Greet greet) {
        String message = greet.getMessage();
        String response = message+"."
          +String.format("Hello from node %s count %s.",id,counter++);
        GreetResponse greetResponse = new
          GreetResponse(greet,response);
        return greetResponse;
    }

}
```

The implementation performs the following tasks:

- It gets the message in the Greet request (provided as an argument)
- It constructs a response by concatenation of the message, the node ID, and a counter
- It wraps the request and response into a GreetResponse object
- It returns the GreetResponse object

To register (bind) this service, we use the OSGi Blueprint.

In the OSGI-INF/blueprint folder of the bundle, we add our blueprint descriptor as follows:

```
<?xml version="1.0" encoding="UTF-8"?>
<blueprint xmlns="http://www.osgi.org/xmlns/blueprint/v1.0.0">

    <!-- Greeter Implementation -->
    <bean id="greeterImpl"
      class="org.apache.karaf.cellar.samples.dosgi.greeter.service.
GreeterImpl">
        <!-- We want the greeter to display the origin of the greet,
          so we use the nodeId -->
```

```
            <argument ref="nodeId"/>
    </bean>

    <!-- The current Node -->
    <bean id="node" factory-ref="clusterManager"
      factory-method="getNode"/>
    <!-- The id of the current node -->
    <bean id="nodeId" factory-ref="node" factory-method="getId"/>

    <!-- OSGi Services  & References -->
    <service ref="greeterImpl"
      interface="org.apache.karaf.cellar.samples.dosgi.greeter.api.
  Greeter">
        <service-properties>
            <entry key="service.exported.interfaces" value="*"/>
        </service-properties>
    </service>

    <reference id="clusterManager"
      interface="org.apache.karaf.cellar.core.ClusterManager"/>

</blueprint>
```

We can see the `service.exported.interfaces` property defined for the
`greeterImpl` service. As we saw earlier, this property is a flag to specify that this
service is available in the cluster. It contains the interface (the service) that we want
to expose to the cluster. In case a bean that provides a service implements multiple
interfaces, we can specify the interface to a user for the cluster interface. The wildcard
(*) means that any interface implemented by the bean will be available in the cluster.

We can now deploy the service bundle on node1.

Cellar DOSGi is not installed by default in the Cellar feature. To enable DOSGi
support, you have to install the `cellar-dosgi` feature with the following command:

```
karaf@root> features:install cellar-dosgi

karaf@root> la|grep -i dosgi

[ 63] [Active    ] [Created    ] [   40] Apache Karaf :: Cellar ::
DOSGi (2.3.1)
```

The first bundle to deploy is the API bundle; this can be done by running the
following command:

```
karaf@root> osgi:install -s
mvn:org.apache.karaf.cellar.samples.dosgi.greeter/org.apache.karaf.
cellar.samples.dosgi.greeter.api/2.3.1
```

Now, we can deploy and start the service bundle with the following command:

```
karaf@root> osgi:install -s
mvn:org.apache.karaf.cellar.samples.dosgi.greeter/org.apache.karaf.
cellar.samples.dosgi.greeter.service/2.3.1
```

We can see our `Greeter` service in the local service registry by running the following command:

```
karaf@root> ls 65
```

```
Apache Karaf :: Cellar :: Samples :: DOSGi Greeter ::
Service (65) provides:
------------------------------------------------------------------------
---
objectClass =
org.apache.karaf.cellar.samples.dosgi.greeter.api.Greeter
osgi.service.blueprint.compname = greeterImpl
service.exported.interfaces = *
service.id = 286
```

We can now see the `service.exported.interface` property that Cellar DOSGi is looking for.

Cellar DOSGi also provides the following `cluster:service-list` command to display the services registered on the cluster (in the distributed service registry):

```
karaf@root> cluster:service-list
Service Class                                            Provider
Node
org.apache.karaf.cellar.samples.dosgi.greeter.api.Greeter    node1:5701
```

We can see our `Greeter` service available in the cluster and provided by node1 of the cluster.

The client bundle

The client bundle provides a `dosgi-greeter:greet` shell command. The shell command is part of the client bundle, and you can find the command code on the GitHub source repository. The command calls the following `GreeterClient`:

```
    package org.apache.karaf.cellar.samples.dosgi.greeter.client;

    import org.apache.karaf.cellar.samples.dosgi.greeter.api.Greet;
```

```java
import
  org.apache.karaf.cellar.samples.dosgi.greeter.api.GreetResponse;
import org.apache.karaf.cellar.samples.dosgi.greeter.api.Greeter;

/**
 * Client that uses a remote Greeter service.
 */
public class GreeterClient {

  private Greeter greeter;
  private String greetMessage;
  private int count;

  public GreeterClient(Greeter greeter, String greetMessage, int
count) {
      this.greeter = greeter;
      this.greetMessage = greetMessage;
      this.count = count;
  }

  public void start() {
      Greet greet  = new Greet(greetMessage);
      for (int i = 0; i < count; i++) {
          GreetResponse greetResponse = greeter.greet(greet);
          if(greetResponse != null) {
              System.out.println(greetResponse.getResponse());
          } else System.out.println("Time out!");
      }
  }

}
```

The client is pretty basic, as the service is injected in the `greeter` attribute using a blueprint as follows:

```xml
<?xml version="1.0" encoding="UTF-8"?>

<blueprint xmlns="http://www.osgi.org/xmlns/blueprint/v1.0.0">

  <reference id="greeter"
    interface="org.apache.karaf.cellar.samples.dosgi.greeter.api.
Greeter"/>

</blueprint>
```

This blueprint descriptor is very simple. It just gets a reference to the `Greeter` service. This reference can be a reference to the local actual service or to a proxy of a remote service.

We can now deploy the API and client bundles on node2 with the following commands:

```
karaf@root> osgi:install -s
mvn:org.apache.karaf.cellar.samples.dosgi.greeter/org.apache.karaf.
cellar.samples.dosgi.greeter.api/2.3.1

karaf@root> osgi:install -s
mvn:org.apache.karaf.cellar.samples.dosgi.greeter/org.apache.karaf.
cellar.samples.dosgi.greeter.client/2.3.1
```

 Node1 and node2 should be in two different groups; otherwise, the installation of the different bundles (API, service, and client) will be spread from one node to another. This is not what we want; we want the service bundle to be installed only on node1 and the client bundle to be installed only on node2.

We can now call the `dosgi-greeter:greet` command as follows:

```
karaf@root> dosgi-greeter:greet hello 5

hello.Hello from node node2 count 0.

hello.Hello from node node2 count 1.

hello.Hello from node node2 count 2.

hello.Hello from node node2 count 3.

hello.Hello from node node2 count 4.
```

Summary

DOSGi is a very simple way to implement remote service communication between nodes. It brings a new dimension to OSGi, and allows you to create large and scalable applications that you can deploy on a farm of a container.

Used in correlation with cluster groups (to target the deployment of the bundles on certain nodes), DOSGi is the first step forward in runtime clustering. It means that Cellar is more than a provisioning clustering solution; it also brings interesting features for runtime clustering.

In the next chapter, we will see another usage of Cellar for runtime clustering when used in combination with Apache Camel.

8
Cellar and Camel

In the previous chapter, we saw that Cellar can act as more than a provisioning cluster solution, providing DOSGi to allow communication between remote bundles.

As Cellar leverages Hazelcast, it could be used by the Camel Hazelcast component. Thanks to this component, it's possible to implement communication between remote Camel routes.

The Camel Hazelcast component can use the Hazelcast instance provided by Cellar. It can use the different distributed resources provided by Hazelcast such as distributed maps, queues, and lists. This offers a large panel of solutions depending on use cases.

The communication between remote routes

In Camel, when you are local to one Karaf instance, you have different ways to use a route from another route as follows:

- The `direct` endpoint is synchronous, which is local to one `CamelContext` (only routes in the same `CamelContext` component can communicate using `direct`).

- The `direct-vm` endpoint is exactly the same as `direct` but global to the JVM. It means that routes from different `CamelContext` can communicate using `direct-vm`.

- The **staged event-driven architecture (SEDA)** endpoint is asynchronous, which is local to one `CamelContext` (only routes in the same `CamelContext` component can communicate using SEDA). A `seda` endpoint (producer) creates a queue (`BlockingQueue`) and pushes messages in this queue. Another `seda` endpoint (consumer) consumes from this queue. A producer and consumer use different threads.

- The vm endpoint is exactly the same as seda but global to the JVM. It means that routes from different CamelContext can communicate using vm.

These components are convenient to implement communication between Camel routes. However, this communication is local to the same JVM.

When we implement a farm or cluster of Karaf instances, it makes sense to deploy Camel routes that are able to communicate with routes from other instances. Thanks to this, we can specialize an instance and delegate parts of the route execution to other instances.

Moreover, as Cellar is a dynamic cluster (it's easy to add a new node in the cluster), it makes sense to leverage multiple nodes to execute routes. Like this, we can implement a dynamic and scalable cluster of Camel routes.

One way to implement such a solution is to use a **Java Message Service** (**JMS**). Using a broker, such as Apache ActiveMQ (or any JMS broker), it's possible for a route to produce a message in a queue in the broker and other routes can consume from the queue. This approach is interesting because we can leverage the features provided by brokers (message persistence, HA, and so on), but this requires the use of an additional middleware resource, the broker. This means that we have to use Cellar to provision the cluster and maintain the broker.

Thanks to Cellar and the Camel Hazelcast component with SEDA, we can implement something similar without the JMS broker. There is no requirement to add an additional middleware (the JMS broker), which will require installation, administration, maintenance, and tuning.

However, some features provided by the JMS broker, especially ActiveMQ, are very interesting, such as master/slave, network of brokers, and persistent store.

In the following diagram, we can see that the Camel route A uses the Hazelcast instance provided by Cellar on **NodeA** (thanks to the camel-hazelcast component). This Camel route A produces a message in a Hazelcast queue. On the other hand, the Camel route B consumes the message in the Hazelcast queue, again thanks to the camel-hazelcast component:

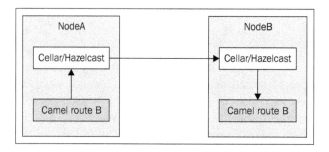

On the first node (**NodeA**), we install Cellar, Camel (`camel-blueprint`), and the `camel-hazelcast` component as follows:

```
karaf@nodeA> features:addurl
mvn:org.apache.karaf.cellar/apache-karaf-cellar/2.3.0/xml/features

karaf@nodeA> features:install cellar

karaf@nodeA> features:addurl
mvn:org.apache.camel.karaf/apache-camel/2.12.0/xml/features

karaf@nodeA> features:install camel-blueprint

karaf@nodeA> features:install camel-hazelcast
```

The node is now ready to deploy Camel routes.

We create a first route using the Camel Blueprint DSL. For that, we create the `route.xml` file as follows:

```xml
<?xml version="1.0" encoding="UTF-8"?>
<blueprint xmlns="http://www.osgi.org/xmlns/blueprint/v1.0.0"
        xmlns:xsi="http://www.w3.org/2001/XMLSchema-instance"
        xsi:schemaLocation="
        http://www.osgi.org/xmlns/blueprint/v1.0.0 http://www.osgi.
org/xmlns/blueprint/v1.0.0/blueprint.xsd">

  <camelContext xmlns="http://camel.apache.org/schema/blueprint">

  <route id="routeA">
     <from uri="timer:simple?period=5000"/>
    <setBody>
         <simple>Hello World</simple>
    </setBody>
     <to uri="hazelcast:seda:myqueue"/>
  </route>

  </camelContext>

</blueprint>
```

This route is pretty simple. Every 5 seconds, it creates a exchange, sets the body of the message to `Hello World`, and sends to a Hazelcast SEDA queue named `myqueue`.

The messages will be stored in a Hazelcast queue waiting for consumers to get messages from this queue. It looks like JMS, but the queue is distributed among all Cellar nodes.

To deploy this route, we just drop the `route.xml` file into the `deploy` folder of **NodeA**.

So, now we have a node that produces messages in a Cellar/Hazelcast queue.

On **NodeB**, we will also install Cellar, Camel (`camel-blueprint`), the `camel-stream` component (to display messages directly on `System.out`), and the `camel-hazelcast` component as follows:

```
karaf@nodeB> features:addurl
mvn:org.apache.karaf.cellar/apache-karaf-cellar/2.3.0/xml/features

karaf@nodeB> features:install cellar

karaf@nodeB> features:addurl
mvn:org.apache.camel.karaf/apache-camel/2.12.0/xml/features

karaf@nodeB> features:install camel-blueprint

karaf@nodeB> features:install camel-hazelcast

karaf@nodeB> features:install camel-stream
```

On **NodeB**, we create a Camel route that will consume the messages from the Cellar/Hazelcast queue.

We define this route using the Camel Blueprint DSL in a `route.xml` file that we drop into the `deploy` folder (of **NodeB**) as follows:

```xml
<?xml version="1.0" encoding="UTF-8"?>
<blueprint xmlns="http://www.osgi.org/xmlns/blueprint/v1.0.0"
           xmlns:xsi="http://www.w3.org/2001/XMLSchema-instance"
           xsi:schemaLocation="
           http://www.osgi.org/xmlns/blueprint/v1.0.0 http://www.osgi.
org/xmlns/blueprint/v1.0.0/blueprint.xsd">

  <camelContext xmlns="http://camel.apache.org/schema/blueprint">

  <route id="routeB">
    <from uri="hazelcast:seda:myqueue"/>
   <to uri="stream:out"/>
  </route>

  </camelContext>

</blueprint>
```

As soon as this route is initiated, we can see the following message in the **NodeB** System.out (directly on the shell console as we use stream:out in the route):

```
Hello World
Hello World
Hello World
Hello World
```

This means that routeB, deployed on **NodeB**, consumes the messages from the myqueue distributed queue. As this queue is a Cellar/Hazelcast distributed queue, the actual data is not local to one node but spread on all nodes of the cluster.

It's also possible to deploy routeB on multiple nodes (for instance, using a specific cluster group with the cluster:feature-install command). In that case, we will have multiple consumers on the same queue, providing a very efficient scalable solution.

Together with the Cellar node discovery mechanism (especially using multicast/unicast), we can very easily add new nodes in the cluster that directly become a consumer or producer (depending on the route that we deploy).

Thanks to the Hazelcast SEDA endpoints provided by the camel-hazelcast component and Cellar, you can easily provide a remote communication solution for your Camel routes.

If we compare Hazelcast SEDA with JMS endpoints, it's very similar. JMS is probably more robust as it leverages all the features provided by the broker (persistence store, conduit subscription, exclusive consumers, and so on). However, for simple remote route communication, without adding additional middleware such as the JMS broker, Hazelcast SEDA is a good solution.

Caching with a distributed map

Another use case for Cellar and camel-hazelcast together is the implementation of a distributed cache solution.

The camel-hazelcast component allows you to use a distributed map and execute different operations on this map.

As it's distributed, it means that the data is spread between different nodes: all nodes can see the same data (entries/values) from the distributed map. This means that you can share data between nodes.

In a Camel route, you can perform the following operations on the distributed map:

- `put`: To add new data in the map
- `delete`: To remove data from the map
- `get`: To retrieve all data from the map
- `query`: To retrieve particular data from the map

The operation type is defined in the `CamelHazelcastOperationType` header.

For instance, we can implement a route that updates the cache with the following code:

```
<route>
  <from uri="direct-vm:add-in-cache"/>
  <setHeader headerName="CamelHazelcastOperationType">
    <constant>put</constant>
  </setHeader>
  <to uri="hazelcast:map:mycache"/>
</route>
```

This route will receive a message on the `direct-vm` endpoint that contains the `CamelHazelcastObjectId` header with an ID as the value and data to store as the message body.

The `hazelcast:map` endpoint will update the `mycache` map with a entry ID/body. On the other hand, a route can get the data from the cache (one dataset if the ID is provided or all data if no ID is provided) as follows:

```
<route>
  <from uri="direct-vm:retrieve-from-cache"/>
  <setHeader headerName="CamelHazelcastOperationType">
    <constant>get</constant>
  </setHeader>
  <to uri="hazelcast:map:mycache"/>
</route>
```

Instead of requesting the cache when we need it (with a `get` or `query` operation), it's also possible to trigger a route as soon as the cache content changes. Like this, we can react to a data change (it's a kind of change data capture). To do this, we can create a route that listens on a given distributed map as follows:

```
<route>
  <from uri="hazelcast:map:mycache"/>
  ...
</route>
```

This route will react as soon as the cache content changes. The `hazelcast:map` endpoint sets some headers to get details about the change, especially the following changes:

- `CamelHazelcastListenerAction`: This contains the action performed on the cache, that is, add, remove, update, or evict

- `CamelHazelcastListenerTime`: This is when the change has been performed

- `CamelHazelcastObjectId`: This is the ID of the object that has changed

- `CamelHazelcastCacheName`: This is the name of the distributed map that has changed

Thanks to the `hazelcast:map` endpoints, you can easily implement a distributed cache mechanism.

Summary

In this chapter, we saw that by leveraging Hazelcast, Cellar offers more than a simple provisioning framework. Combined with Camel, it's a good solution to spread your execution logic over multiple nodes and to implement a fully-scalable and distributed system. It brings more flexibility to Camel in terms of provisioning and executing the routes in a clustered environment.

The `camel-hazelcast` component provides other data structures than the ones introduced in this chapter. You can find details on the component documentation at `http://camel.apache.org/hazelcast-component.html`.

In the next chapter, we will see new directions and features for preparation in Cellar, providing even more clustering solutions.

9
Roadmap

In the previous chapters, we saw that Cellar is more than just a simple provisioning cluster that provides advanced features (such as DOSGi) or leverages other projects (such as Camel).

Cellar's aim is to provide more runtime features. These new features can be grouped into the following three categories:

- **HTTP**: Cellar will be used by the Karaf HTTP layer to deal with the clustering of the deployed web applications
- **Monitoring**: Cellar will be used by the Karaf log and JMX service to provide a global monitoring solution for the cluster
- **Other projects**: Cellar can be used to run projects in Karaf, such as ActiveMQ, Camel, and CXF, to provide clustering features on top of these projects

This chapter introduces the new forthcoming features in HTTP and monitoring categories.

HTTP load balancing and session clustering

Karaf directly leverages Pax Web to provide a complete WebContainer service.

With the installation of the `war` feature using the following command, Karaf gets full support from the web bundle thanks to the Jetty web container and Pax Web:

```
karaf@root> features:install war
```

It's now possible to deploy a web application containing servlet for instance.

Karaf WebConsole is a web application. You can install the `webconsole` feature with the following command:

```
karaf@root> features:install webconsole
```

With `webconsole`, you have the Karaf WebConsole available on `http://localhost:8181/system/console`.

Cellar deals with the HTTP layer to provide load balancing and session clustering.

Load balancing

Due to the Cellar cluster provisioning, a web bundle will be deployed on different nodes.

For instance, a web bundle binds and exposes an HTTP servlet on `/service`, which is related to the HTTP service local to each node.

This means we have:

- For node A, the servlet available at `http://A:8181/service`, where A is the hostname or IP address of node A
- For node B, the servlet available at `http://B:8181/service`, where B is the hostname or IP address of node B

Using a browser, a client can connect to node A using `http://A:8181/service` or node B using `http://B:8181/service`. Now, imagine that we deploy only to B using `http://B:8181/service` (for instance, using a dedicated cluster group). It will be great for clients to use `http://A:8181/service`, even if the service is not actually deployed on A. Cellar will act as a proxy from A to B (where the service is available).

Now, imagine we have three nodes: A, B, and C. The service is deployed on node A (using `http://A:8181/service`) and node B (using `http://B:8181/service`). Node C doesn't have the service deployed, but it can act as a load balancer to the service on nodes A and B. This means that a client would be able to use `http://C:8181/service` and Cellar will load balance and proxy the HTTP requests to `http://A:8181/service` and `http://B:8181/service` (for instance, using round robin, random, or weight-based algorithms defined in the Cellar configuration). This concept is explained in the following diagram:

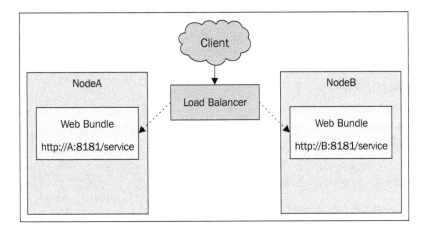

The load balancer can be:

- A hardware load balancer (Cisco, Juniper, F5, and so on)
- A software load balancer (for instance, using the `mod_proxy_balancer` module with Apache HTTPd)

The solution of using such an external load balancer is a classic one, but we may face the following two issues with these load balancers:

- This requires an additional middleware: the load balancer.
- The configuration of the load balancer is static. If we add new nodes, we have to manually update the load balancer configuration.

As Cellar is a very dynamic clustering solution, it's very easy to add new nodes. Thanks to the discovery service, Cellar knows when and where a servlet is registered.

Cellar will store the list of nodes providing a servlet URL. It's stored in a Hazelcast-distributed map.

The map will look as follows:

- `/service1: nodeA, nodeB, nodeC`
- `/service2: nodeB, nodeC`

The Cellar HTTP service will act as a proxy from the local node to other nodes.

The Cellar HTTP service looks like the DOSGi service. On a local node, Cellar creates a proxy servlet for each servlet that is registered (`/service1` and `/service2`). If a client sends an HTTP request to the node, the proxy servlet will proxy/forward the request to the nodes, where the actual servlet has been deployed. This is shown in the following diagram:

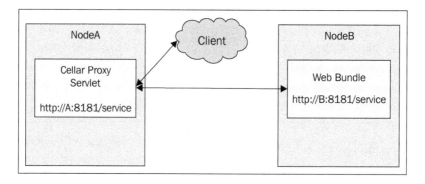

Pax Web registers an OSGi service when a servlet is deployed. Cellar will provide a service listener on the servlet's service. This listener will store the servlets in a cluster map like the following:

- `URI = node, node`

This means we will have `/service = nodeB` for instance.

On all nodes, Cellar will create a proxy servlet for all URIs contained in the cluster map if the actual URI is not already present. For instance, Cellar will create a proxy servlet for `/service` on node A but not on node B (as the actual `/service` is located).

If a client calls on `http://A:8181/service`, this will use the Cellar proxy servlet that will proxy an HTTP request and respond to node B as described in the cluster map.

The cluster map will be able to contain multiple nodes for one URI. For instance, `/service` may be deployed and available on nodes B, C, and D. In that case, Cellar will use a round robin, or random algorithm to choose the target node to proxy to. The algorithm will be defined by a configuration.

This load balancing feature will be available as an optional feature `cellar-http-loadbalancer` with its own configuration file.

Session clustering

A web application can use a client session to identify the requests coming from the same clients. Used in a cluster environment, in order to work, we have to use session affinity. Once the client has sent a request to a node, this client has to send the next request to the same node. The issue is that if the node fails, the client session is lost and so is all the work in progress.

Instead of session affinity, Cellar will provide support for session clustering. This means that the HTTP sessions of each node are replicated to all the other nodes. Thanks to that, we can load balance each request from any client to any node, as all nodes store all HTTP sessions.

To provide this feature, Cellar directly leverages a feature provided by Hazelcast (`http://www.hazelcast.com/use-cases/web-session-clustering/`).

Hazelcast provides a servlet filter that intercepts the HTTP requests to update the session distributed map.

Normally, the developer has to update the web application `web.xml` to explicitly add the Hazelcast filter with the following code:

```
<filter>
 <filter-name>hazelcast-filter</filter-name>
 <filter-class>com.hazelcast.web.WebFilter</filter-class>
 <!-
    Name of the distributed map storing
    your web session objects
 ->
 <init-param>
    <param-name>map-name</param-name>
    <param-value>my-sessions</param-value>
 </init-param>
 <init-param>
    <param-name>sticky-session</param-name>
    <param-value>true</param-value>
 </init-param>
 <!-
    Are you debugging? Default is false.
 ->
 <init-param>
    <param-name>debug</param-name>
    <param-value>true</param-value>
 </init-param>
</filter>
```

```
<filter-mapping>
    <filter-name>hazelcast-filter</filter-name>
    <url-pattern>/*</url-pattern>
    <dispatcher>FORWARD</dispatcher>
    <dispatcher>INCLUDE</dispatcher>
    <dispatcher>REQUEST</dispatcher>
</filter-mapping>
<listener>
    <listener-class>com.hazelcast.web.SessionListener</listener-class>
</listener>
```

As Pax Web registers each servlet as an OSGi service, Cellar will provide a servlet service listener to dynamically add a servlet filter on top of the actual filter.

The cluster session will be available as an optional feature `cellar-http-session` that the user will have to install.

Clustering a log service

Karaf provides a very rich logging service by leveraging Pax logging.

It's possible to change the log level or display the log messages directly in the Karaf shell console using specific commands: `log:set`, `log:get`, and `log:display`.

Cellar will provide the `cellar-log` optional feature. The installation of this feature will add a new log appender. This appender will store the log messages in a cluster map node/message.

Thanks to this cluster map, from any node we will be able to see log messages on other nodes by issuing the following command:

karaf@root> cluster:log-display

nodeA ...

nodeA ...

nodeB ...

nodeA ...

For a specific node, run the following command:

karaf@root> cluster:log-display nodeA

nodeA ...

nodeA ...

The purpose is to provide a cluster form of the `log:*` commands.

For instance, it is possible to change the log levels of all nodes in the cluster with the following command:

```
karaf@root> cluster:log-set DEBUG
```

For a specific node, run the following command:

```
karaf@root> cluster:log-set DEBUG nodeA
```

The future versions of Cellar will be more than version updates. They will provide new cluster features, first on the HTTP service, and other convenient features.

Even the version updates will be very important, especially with the support of new Hazelcast versions.

Summary

This chapter showed the future of Cellar. One of the key directions for Cellar is to provide more runtime features. If provisioning and synchronization were the primary purposes, Cellar now provides more advanced features. If in this chapter we saw the upcoming HTTP and log cluster features, the roadmap is still open. The relationship between Cellar and other projects (such as CXF, ActiveMQ, or Camel, as we saw with Pax Web) will certainly provide interesting runtime features.

Cellar will be the most complete open source cluster solution for Karaf platforms, providing both cluster provisioning as it does now, as well as runtime clustering.

Index

A

Apache Karaf
  features 11-16
  provisioning 13, 14
Apache Karaf Cellar
  about 21
  architecture 24
  commands 26
  features 24
  installing 26
  URL, for information 21
Apache Karaf locking mechanism 18
Apache ZooKeeper 22
API bundle 79-81
architecture, Apache Karaf Cellar 24
async backup operations 43

B

backup
  about 42, 43
  persistence 43
blacklisted filter 71
blacklist keyword 71
bundle cluster event 70, 72
BundleEventHandler 65
bundles, Cluster resources 27-29
bundles, targeting provisioning 55, 56

C

caching
  with distributed map 91-93
Camel 87

camel-hazelcast component 91
Cellar
  runtime features 95
Cellar core 25
Cellar distributed map 42
Cellar Distributed OSGi (Cellar DOSGi) 77
cellar-eventadmin feature 36, 58
cellar-obr feature 37, 58
Cellar sources
  URL, for source code 79
cellar-webconsole feature 37
client bundle 78, 84-86
ClusterBundleEvent 63
cluster:bundle-install command 28
cluster:bundle-list command 27
cluster component
  purpose 23
ClusterConfigEvent 63
cluster:config-list command 33
cluster:config-propset command 35
cluster:consumer-start command 64
cluster:consumer-status command 64
cluster:consumer-stop command 64
cluster event consumer
  about 61-63
  functionalities 64
Cluster event consumer and handlers
      module 25
ClusterEventHandler 65
cluster event model 23
cluster event producer
  about 61, 62
  functions 62
Cluster event producer module 25

cluster events
  bundle 70, 72
  config 70, 73
  features 70-74
  filtering 69, 70
  inbound 71
  outbound 71
  specifying 71
cluster events, for producer
  ClusterBundleEvent 63
  ClusterConfigEvent 63
  ClusterFeatureEvent 63
  ClusterObrEvent 63
ClusterFeatureEvent 63
cluster:feature-install command 54
cluster:feature-install <group_name>
      <feature_name> command 54
cluster:group-create command 70
cluster:group-create <group-name>
      command 51
cluster:group-delete <group_name>
      command 52
cluster:group-join command
  about 52, 53
  arguments 52
cluster:group-list command 52
cluster:group-quit command 53
cluster groups
  managing 51-53
cluster:group-set command 53
cluster:handler-start command 66
cluster:handler-status command 65
cluster:handler-stop command 65
clustering
  layers 22
Cluster Manager cluster 22
cluster manager component 22
cluster:node-list command 26
ClusterObrEvent 63
cluster:producer-start command 63
cluster:producer-status command 62
cluster:producer-stop command 62, 63
Cluster resources
  about 27
  bundles 27-29
  configuration 33-35
  Karaf features 30-32

Karaf WebConsole plugin 37
  optional resources 36, 37
Cluster topologies 21, 22
commands module 25
commands, Apache Karaf Cellar 26
commands, targeting provisioning 59, 60
commons-lang bundle 28, 29
communication
  between remote routes 87-91
config:list command 73
configuration, Cluster resources 33-35
ConfigurationEventHandler 65
configuration, filters 69, 70
configurations, targeting provisioning 57

D

default filter configuration 75
distributed cluster resource states
  about 40
  Cellar distributed map 42
  distributed queues 41
  distributed topics 41
distributed map
  caching with 91-93
distributed queues 41
distributed topics 41
dosgi-greeter:greet shell command 84

E

event handlers
  BundleEventHandler 65
  ClusterEventHandler 65
  ConfigurationEventHandler 65
  FeaturesEventHandler 65
  ObrBundleEventHandler 65
  ObrUrlEventHandler 65
  overview 64-66
event identifier 72

F

features, Apache Karaf Cellar 24
features cluster event 70, 74
FeaturesEventHandler 65
features:install <feature_name>
      command 54

features:list command 74
features, targeting provisioning 54, 55
filters
    configuring 69, 70
functionalities, cluster event consumer 64
functions, cluster event producer 62

G

greet() method 79
GreetResponse class 80

H

Hazelcast
    about 24, 25, 39, 40
    URL, for session clustering 99
hazelcast:map endpoint, headers
    about 93
    CamelHazelcastCacheName 93
    CamelHazelcastListenerAction 93
    CamelHazelcastListenerTime 93
    CamelHazelcastObjectId 93
Hazelcast NIO
    about 78
    URL 78
HTTP
    load balancing 95-98
    session clustering 95, 99, 100

I

inbound cluster events 71
installation, Apache Karaf Cellar 26
IPv6 support 48

J

Java Authentication and Authorization
        Service (JAAS) 12
Java Database Connectivity (JDBC) 13
Java JAR (Java ARchive) file 9
Java Message Service (JMS) 13, 88
Java Naming and Directory Interface
        (JNDI) 13
Java NIO Javadocs
    URL 78

Java Persistence API (JPA) 13
Java Transaction API (JTA) 13
Java Virtual Machine (JVM) 8

K

Karaf features, Cluster resources 30-32
Karaf WebConsole plugin, Cluster
        resources 37

L

layers, clustering 22
listeners 67
load balancing, HTTP 96-98
log service
    clustering 100, 101

M

MBeans 25
modules, Karaf
    Cellar core 25
    Cluster event consumer and handlers 25
    Cluster event producer 25
    Commands 25
    Hazelcast 25
    MBeans 25
    Resources listeners 25
    Resources synchronizers 25
    WebConsole plugin 25
multiple Apache Karaf containers
    about 17, 18
    provisioning cluster 19

N

networks
    about 44
    encryption, enabling of content 47
    interfaces 45, 46
    IPv6 support 48, 49
    multiple clusters 44
    outbound ports, restricting 49
    SSL 46
    TCP/IP 45

nodes
  communicating, via distributed
    service registry 78
  NodeA 88, 89
  NodeB 90, 91
none keyword 72

O

OBR 15, 58
ObrBundleEventHandler 65
ObrUrlEventHandler 65
Open Software Gateway initiative.
    See OSGi
optional resources, Cluster resources 36, 37
optional resources, targeting
    provisioning 57, 58
org.apache.felix.fileinstall:
    configurations 73
org.apache.karaf.cellar: configurations 73
org.apache.karaf.management
    configuration 73
org.apache.karaf.shell configuration 73
org.ops4j.pax.logging configuration 73
org.ops4j.pax.web configuration 73
OSGi
  about 8
  agility 8
  discovery 8
  features 8
  framework 8
  purposes 8
  reuse 8
  visibility 8
OSGi bundle
  about 9
  dependency 9, 10
OSGi Bundle Repository. *See* OBR
OSGi container
  about 11
  Apache Karaf features 15
  OBR 15
  provisioning, in Apache Karaf 13
outbound cluster events 71
outbound ports
  restricting 49
overlap, targeting provisioning 58, 59

P

Pluggable Authentication Modules
    (PAM) 12
provisioning cluster, Apache Karaf
  tasks 19

R

regular expression (regex) 72
remote routes
  communication 87-91
replicas
  about 42, 43
  persistence 43
resources 70
Resources listeners module 25
Resources synchronizers module 25
Role Based Access Control
    (RBAC) system 12
runtime features, Cellar
  HTTP 95
  monitoring 95
  other projects 95

S

service bundle 78, 81-84
Service-Oriented Architecture (SOA) 10, 77
session clustering, HTTP 99, 100
SSL socket communication 46
staged event-driven architecture (SEDA) 87
sync backup operations 43
synchronizers 67

T

targeting provisioning
  about 53
  bundles 55, 56
  commands, summary 59, 60
  configurations 57
  features 54, 55
  optional resources 57, 58
  overlapping 58, 59
TCP/IP 45
time to live (TTL) 41

W

Web Application Bundle (WAB) 13
WebConsole plugin 25
whitelisted filter 71
whitelist keyword 71

Thank you for buying
Learning Karaf Cellar

About Packt Publishing

Packt, pronounced 'packed', published its first book "*Mastering phpMyAdmin for Effective MySQL Management*" in April 2004 and subsequently continued to specialize in publishing highly focused books on specific technologies and solutions.

Our books and publications share the experiences of your fellow IT professionals in adapting and customizing today's systems, applications, and frameworks. Our solution based books give you the knowledge and power to customize the software and technologies you're using to get the job done. Packt books are more specific and less general than the IT books you have seen in the past. Our unique business model allows us to bring you more focused information, giving you more of what you need to know, and less of what you don't.

Packt is a modern, yet unique publishing company, which focuses on producing quality, cutting-edge books for communities of developers, administrators, and newbies alike. For more information, please visit our website: www.packtpub.com.

About Packt Open Source

In 2010, Packt launched two new brands, Packt Open Source and Packt Enterprise, in order to continue its focus on specialization. This book is part of the Packt Open Source brand, home to books published on software built around Open Source licenses, and offering information to anybody from advanced developers to budding web designers. The Open Source brand also runs Packt's Open Source Royalty Scheme, by which Packt gives a royalty to each Open Source project about whose software a book is sold.

Writing for Packt

We welcome all inquiries from people who are interested in authoring. Book proposals should be sent to author@packtpub.com. If your book idea is still at an early stage and you would like to discuss it first before writing a formal book proposal, contact us; one of our commissioning editors will get in touch with you.

We're not just looking for published authors; if you have strong technical skills but no writing experience, our experienced editors can help you develop a writing career, or simply get some additional reward for your expertise.

OSGi and Apache Felix 3.0 Beginner's Guide

ISBN: 978-1-84951-138-4   Paperback: 336 pages

Build your very own OSGi applications using the flexible and powerful Felix Framework

1. Build a completely operational real-life application composed of multiple bundles and a web frontend using Felix.

2. Get yourself acquainted with the OSGi concepts, in an easy-to-follow progressive manner.

3. Learn everything needed about the Felix Framework and get familiar with Gogo, its command-line shell to start developing your OSGi applications.

Instant Apache ServiceMix How-to

ISBN: 978-1-84951-966-3   Paperback: 66 pages

Learn to create simple ServiceMix-based integration solutions using short, practical, hands-on recipes

1. Learn something new in an Instant! A short, fast, focused guide delivering immediate results.

2. Leverage OSGI to speed up the ESB deployment.

3. Define message flow with Camel DSL.

4. Expose your system via web services.

www.ingramcontent.com/pod-product-compliance
Lightning Source LLC
LaVergne TN
LVHW081346050326
832903LV00024B/1347